Tragedies turn into triumph in the hands of the Maker

A Grieving Heart
is Most Loved

Second Edition

Dr. Li Sze Chow, Ph.D.

ISBN: 978-967-18261-1-9

Published by
Li Sze Chow
Desa Setapak
Kuala Lumpur
Malaysia
Email: lisze.chow@gmail.com

Contents

Forewords

As I read this book, I remember Mary Magdalene of the Bible, who loved Jesus very much because she had been forgiven much. She had so much humility because she had been loved much. Mary Magdalene appeared in all the four gospels. She found healing at the feet of Jesus, where she anointed Jesus' feet with her tears. She was a witness at the foot of the cross, an attendant at Jesus' burial, and the first person to hear the words of the newly risen Lord. *"Therefore, I tell you, her many sins have been forgiven – as her great love has shown. But whoever has been forgiven little loves little."* (Luke 7:47) This verse speaks of Li Sze. Those who are forgiven much, love much. God's grace is an unspeakably precious reality in Li Sze that has changed her and inspired her great love for God. It is very glaring to me. Her love for God is astounding. Jesus says that in this world, we will have trials and tribulations but we are to be of good cheer for He has overcome the world (John 16:33).

Corrie ten Boom once said, *"If you look at the world, you will be distressed; if you look within, you will be depressed; if you look at Christ, you will be at rest."* Ever since evil and sin entered the world, nothing has worked perfectly. Everything on this planet is broken. Our nature is broken, economy is broken, the air and water are polluted, friendship is broken, relationship is broken, our body is broken, and plans are broken. Sin and evil have broken everything on this planet. But what the devil means for evil, God will turn it around for good. God promises to walk through our trials with us. Neither for a minute nor any moment will I forsaken! That is who our God is! Our God is a great and awesome God. Hallelujah! To the One who deserves all our adoration, praises and glory.

Pastor Jennie Seet @ Chong Siew Wah

Co-founder GCC Group of School

It is my privilege to know Dr. Li Sze Chow and witnessed her growth and transformation in God. This book, *A Grieving Heart is Most Loved*, is written from her personal painful experiences of losses and grief. She shares her raw emotions and her vulnerability to glorify God and to help others who are in grief. Truly, it is a remarkable journey of aloneness with many struggles and if God is not for her, her life would have been doomed. As her story unfolds, one cannot help but admire her strong devotion to her two children, which is not often seen in the world today. It is extremely tough for Li Sze as a single mother but she believes in a great God who has been so real to her. Therefore, this book will serve as a good encourager to us not to give up, but to press on in the Lord. It is a good reminder that many believers look to their church for guidance and answers to their problems. Today, the church must not forget to care for the poor and the fatherless.

Pastor Dr. Wong Moi Lee
Former English TEE Director
Seminary Theology Malaysia (STM)

This is a story from the heart, we see the display of despair and grace, hope and disappointment, but in the end, the Glory of God triumphs as despair and disappointment are replaced by courage and strength. This is a story of an ordinary woman in her quest for the meaning of life.

This beautiful story tells us of how our everyday life is woven into the greater story of God. A story like this will grip our hearts, waking us up to the reality of life with an assurance that this must be God working in the life of ordinary people like you and me. This story will challenge you to walk in faith, trusting the Lord as you take every footstep in life in the purview of His grace.

Pastor Eric Mau

Congregation Pastor

Christ Lutheran Church

Acknowledgements

My heartfelt appreciation to everyone who walked with me through the darkest hours in the valley. Without you, it would have been even harder for me to fight all the battles on my own. Your continuous prayer support and words of encouragement have truly comforted me, especially during the sickness and death of my son, Zhen Kan.

I sincerely acknowledge all the pastors who have encouraged me, prayed for me, and supported me in many ways. I am very grateful to my church pastors – Pastor Francis Ho, Pastor Jennie Seet, Pastor Eric Mau, and Pastor Philip Tan – for your continuous prayer and spiritual support. I am grateful to my spiritual lecturers in Seminary Theology Malaysia, Dr Alex Tang and Dr Wong Moi Lee, for the courses that helped me through my grief and discernment of life. I am also grateful to Pastor Bill Wilson, who is my role model in faith and in action. Finally, I am grateful to *you*, my reader, for buying my book and reading it now.

Above all, I am extremely grateful to God. He is the divine Author of this book, *A Grieving Heart is Most Loved*, of which I am His co-author. I am honored to be chosen at this time to be the servant of the Most High God, Yahweh! Praise the Lord for this wonderful work that belongs to Him!

Li Sze Chow

Preface

Jesus looked out for me during the darkest of the darkest hours in my life when my son was critically ill, my daughter was emotionally troubled, and I was divorced! I was at the end of the rope, without hope and numb. I am highly educated, with a PhD degree from a top UK university but my son's illness brought me down low. If it hadn't been for his illness, I would have been too stubborn to even listen to what people say about Jesus. When my son was terminally ill, I tried all religions, all doctors (both Western and traditional) and all alternative therapies. After braving through a torrent of trials, I finally concluded that Jesus is the only Way and the Truth and the Life (John 14:6). Finally, I found the one true God of this universe who created my inmost being and knitted me together in my mother's womb (Psalm 139:13). I am called to belong to Jesus Christ (Romans 1:6) and have followed Him since 2014.

The journey of writing this book has been intensely emotional as I recalled afresh all the pain and agony that I went through with my beloved son, Zhen Kan. I started writing this book in 2015 and concluded it in 2020. There were many times when I put the book aside, and there were times when I didn't know how to end it. But towards the end of 2019, I felt a strong call from the Lord to finish the book, and He even gave me the title *A Grieving Heart is Most Loved.* Writing this book over the course of five years has been a journey of diminishing pain – at first, it felt like salt was rubbed into an open wound, then on a recovering wound, and finally on a nearly recovered wound. Since I have dedicated myself as a living sacrifice for God, I was willing to re-live the pain. Yes! I was willing and I rejoice that I wrote this book to encourage you.

This book is the second edition. During the printing of the first edition, I encountered an unexpected huge financial loss but I did not allow the tragedy to abort this "baby". I sold a gold bracelet, which gave me the exact amount to print 300 copies. By divine appointment, the book launch fell on Sunday, August 30, 2020 – the death anniversary of my son. It was the day to fulfil the promise of God in Isaiah 61:3, *"to all who mourn, God will restore beauty for ashes, joy instead of mourning, and praise instead of despair."* Praise the Lord that the first 300 copies were sold out within three weeks! God has answered my prayer to reach out to 300 people and more.

After this, God spoke to me to add two more chapters. I have added a chapter on *"Loss vs Blessing"* about my career loss and financial loss, and the blessing of a new career. This book would not be complete without a chapter on *"Forgiveness"*, as the Lord has forgiven us. It is a key to freedom, healing and blessings. In these two chapters, you will see the experiences of Job and the Samaritan woman in my life. I have rewritten the last chapter *"Most Loved"* to share about the discernment of life and the baton of faith.

The cover of this book was personally designed by myself after I saw a vision of a very broken heart (mine) being embraced and surrounded by a much bigger heart to symbolise God's love that soothes my inner heart. I chose a yellow background to represent joy, as it reminds me to *"Rejoice always"* (1 Thessalonians 5:16) and *"Do not grieve, for the joy of the LORD is your strength."* (Nehemiah 8:10)

I pray that you will be encouraged and moved by my heart-wrenching stories, with the everlasting arms of God embracing me tightly. You will see the unfailing love of Christ, His unchanging faithfulness, His amazing grace, His wonderful favour and His mighty power in the midst of all my pain, loss, grief, disappointment and hardships. God is the Author of this book; I am His co-author. To God be the glory!

Li Sze Chow

Introduction

I have asked the Holy Spirit to give me the grace to empathise with Li Sze's personal life experiences, which she describes as a broken life plus a broken heart in a living hell. I have prayed for God's mercy upon her since the day I saw her and Zhen Kan in the paediatric ward at University Malaya Medical Centre. My wife, Christine, and I asked for her permission to share Christ's love and to pray for God's grace and peace.

"And we know that for those who love God all things work together for good, for those who are called according to his purpose. For those whom he foreknew he also predestined to be conformed to the image of his Son, in order that he might be the firstborn among many brothers. And those whom he predestined he also called, and those whom he called he also justified, and those whom he justified he also glorified." Romans 8:28-30 (ESV)

Some of us at Christ Lutheran Church have walked with Li Sze through the time of her anxiety, which words cannot fully express. I knew that the Lord Himself would guide her through those dark hours of tribulation, restore her dignity and destine her for greatness in His Name. With zeal in prayer and ministry, Li Sze has grown in her spiritual walk. Praise the Lord for the grace of transformation from ash to beauty in her and Nina.

"I have said these things to you, that in me you may have peace. In the world you will have tribulation. But take heart; I have overcome the world." John 16:33 (ESV)

In the pages of Li Sze's life story in this book, you will find the unfailing love of God in bringing salvation to the soul of a desperate woman and mother seeking the meaning and purpose of life. In His wisdom and grace, the God of mercy and compassion will save and deliver those who call upon the Name of Jesus from darkness into His wonderful light.

"But you are a chosen race, a royal priesthood, a holy nation, a people for his own possession, that you may proclaim the excellencies of him who called you out of darkness into his marvelous light. Once you were not a people, but now you are God's people; once you had not received mercy, but now you have received mercy." 1 Peter 2:9-10 (ESV)

I pray that all those who read this testimony of God's grace in the life of Li Sze will find victory for their own struggles in life.

"Come to me, all who labor and are heavy laden, and I will give you rest. Take my yoke upon you, and learn from me, for I am gentle and lowly in heart, and you will find rest for your souls. For my yoke is easy, and my burden is light." Matthew 11:28-30 (ESV)

Reverend Francis Ho
Lutheran Church Malaysia
Christ Lutheran Church

A Grieving Heart is Most Loved

Chapter 1

Broken Life

Background

I grew up in a staunch Buddhist family, with parents who believed in Nichiren Daishonin Buddhism and practised the faith with an organisation called Soka Gakkai Malaysia (SGM). My mother and the Buddhist leaders taught me a lot of the good moral values and philosophies in Buddhism. I thought I had the best religion and was a faithful Buddhist. When I was 12 years old, I started chanting every day, sometimes for over an hour. My record was chanting for 10 hours in a day, praying for my heart's desire to be fulfilled. The meditation was good. However, deep down, there was this inner void that left me with many unanswered questions.

From young, I had always studied and worked very hard, and therefore achieved sterling results. I'd always thought that all my achievements were from my Buddhist beliefs and chanting. I completed the Grade 8 ABRSM Piano examination and hold a diploma in pianoforte from the London College of Music (LCM). I entered the University of Malaya with 5 straight As in STPM (Malaysia Pre-University Examination) and completed the B.Eng. Telecommunication Engineering Degree with first-class honours. It seemed to me then that all my hard work had paid off. After a year of working in the industry, I got the opportunity to further my studies in M.Sc. Data Communication, followed by a PhD in Electrical and Electronic Engineering in The University of Sheffield, UK. I got a partial scholarship and worked part-time to support myself without any financial help from my parents. They were very proud of me and I was also very proud to have achieved all these by myself.

It never crossed my mind that my intelligence and diligence were actually gifts from God because I did not know Him then. At that point, what I had learned in life, school, home, and Buddhism was that the route to achieving my desires was hard work. With this philosophy, I worked extremely hard until I got my PhD in the UK. However, I easily succumbed to the rat race, chasing after the things of the world. Disappointment soon assailed me when I realised this was an unfair world. Many times, I did not get what I wanted no matter how hard I worked. It seemed that nothing in this world could really satisfy me, and I became restless, melancholic and empty without really knowing why. Chanting only gave me short-term respite, and I soon gave in to the irresistible allure of the world again.

Broken Marriage

Mr. L (pseudonym) was a handsome Brazilian man, two years younger than I. Marrying him wasn't about true love; I was simply compelled to follow the social norm – get married, raise a family. I didn't want to lose out by staying single and getting laughed at by friends and relatives. We tied the knot after dating for less than a year. It was an immature decision because we didn't know each other well. Love is blind! Soon after our marriage, I was dumbstruck by his immaturity and many weaknesses that I found unacceptable. I thought I was able to or had the ability to change him, but all my efforts were futile.

I was working full-time to support the family financially while he was doing his PhD in the UK. I used up all my savings to pay the deposit for a house in Chesterfield so that we could start a family. He had zero savings even though he was already 30 years old. Daily, he would complain about the people around him, including his parents. Right after I gave birth to our first child, Nina, he managed to get a job in London. I gave up my job in Sheffield and we moved there. It was a big sacrifice that turned into a big shock when he decided to quit his job two months later. He told me to return to my job in Sheffield because he simply could not cope with his job and support the family financially in London. He had been a spendthrift from young and had no proper financial planning. Our expenditure was more than his income. In short, he was not mature enough to start a family and support the family financially. I did not know how to change him and live with him. Helpless and in despair, I thought of returning to Malaysia with Nina but I did not because I wanted Nina to grow up with a father, to have a "complete" family. So, I relented and we returned to Sheffield. Fortunately, my ex-supervisor was kind enough to reinstate my position as a post-doctorate Research Associate in The University of Sheffield. I was working full-time again to support the family while he took care of Nina at home. He couldn't get any job and we struggled financially. A few months later, his parents asked us to move to Brazil where they could support us. Hoping for a better family life, we all moved back to Brazil in July 2010. Nina was only 9 months old. Once again, I had to give up my job in The University of Sheffield. We lost our semi-detached house in Chesterfield, sold our brand new Citroen Exclusive car and all the furniture in the house. We lost everything that we had built in the UK. What a sacrifice!

Back in Brazil, our relationship did not improve but got worse instead due to many factors, including the vast cultural and lifestyle differences. I was not happy at all and we argued a lot, mainly over money. We tried to resolve our problems but in the end, the marriage just did not work out. The day after he and Nina were baptised in a Catholic church, he told me that it was the end and there was nothing left between us. He wanted a divorce. I was 3 months into my second pregnancy and that was the time I needed him most. I knelt before him and begged him to give me another chance. That was the darkest time in my life because I was all alone in Brazil without any relatives or close friends. I did not have a job as I could not speak Portuguese. He had refused to teach me Portuguese and instead, insisted we spoke English as he wanted to practise speaking English. What a selfish man! I did not have much money and my parents were in Malaysia. My father, who had objected to the marriage from the start, had disagreed with my decision to move to Brazil. I thought I could share the sorrows of my divorce and my second pregnancy with them. Instead, I was slapped with another disappointment when my mother advised me to abort the child. I knew I couldn't abort my baby no matter how difficult it was. Before having Nina, I had a miscarriage and experienced the sorrows of a miscarriage. Some Catholic Christians prayed for me even though I was still a Buddhist. Nobody told me about Jesus then and I continued chanting the Buddhist Daimoku mantra. I was crying every day during that pregnancy, and often woke up at night, worrying about my future.

One day, Mr. L forced me out from his parents' home and took away the house keys from me. The worst thing was that he took Nina with him. I was out of the house, pregnant, sitting on the street, head bent low, staring at the floor. I looked up to the sky. I did not know who I could pray to, and I did not know what to do. I did not know how long I sat on the street, crying alone. Then, a friend of theirs named Mary passed by and took me to a shop for a talk. At least there was someone nice and willing to help me. She brought me to a gynecologist for a check-up and introduced a lawyer to settle the divorce. According to the Brazilian divorce law, the mother will usually get custody of the children – unless she is a prostitute or insane. Imagine my horror when Mr. L told the court during the hearing that I was insane and the baby in my womb was not his! Thankfully, the judge did not believe him. Justice was dispensed when I got custody of my daughter. At that time, I was staying at a flat belonging to Mr. L's parents, who were utterly disappointed with their son. Tragedy struck again when I received a legal letter from them, demanding that I vacate the flat. Why? After all, I was pregnant with their grandchild and looking after their granddaughter Nina. Mr. L must have incited them to kick me out of their flat with his petty lies.

Another lawyer offered to help me get a court's authorisation to bring Nina back to Malaysia. I had no other place to go to except to return to Malaysia to stay with my parents. Amazingly, this lawyer did not charge me a single cent. After a few months of battling, I finally got the authorisation from the judge. As soon as we got the letter from the judge, my friend helped me to buy the flight ticket to depart the very next day. Fearing that my ex-husband would stop us from leaving, we left without telling him. Thankfully, I managed to meet the travel restriction for pregnant travellers and boarded the plane when I was in my 28th week of pregnancy. The day Nina and I left Brazil was a sad, sad day. I cried… and cried… and cried alone… I felt terribly sad taking my daughter very far away from her father, probably never to meet again. Nina was just over a year old. She was sitting on my lap, next to the baby in my womb. Though I managed to get someone to travel with us, at least to help me with the luggage, I felt I was all alone and fearful of the unknown future ahead of me. Sitting in the plane with Nina and all the people around me, I was oblivious to the hustle bustle around me. The loneliness and pain were unimaginable. The whole journey, including a few stops, took more than 30 hours and I was thankful that my water bag did not burst. In August 2011, we were safely back in Malaysia.

Back in Malaysia

When I arrived in Malaysia, a more daunting challenge awaited me. I had left Malaysia for nine years. Everything had changed. My parents were older and different now. I was very sad that my parents, who had been so proud of me before, had become very disappointed with me instead. They were ashamed of my divorce and couldn't face our relatives, friends and neighbours. In the Chinese culture, it is really shameful to be divorced and come home pregnant. I could feel the neighbors laughing behind my back, accusing me of carrying the child of another man and thus getting divorced by my husband.

Nina was only 21 months old. She did not understand what was going on, but she knew that she had lost something very precious in her life. To make matters worse, raising children in Brazil is completely different from the Chinese way. When she cried and demanded her way, she did not get the love and attention that she used to get in Brazil from her father and grandparents. Truth is, nobody likes a wailing, cranky child here. Furthermore, she looked like her father, whom my parents loathed because he had destroyed their daughter's happiness. It was heartbreaking to see that my parents did not like Nina either and I often quarreled with them over her. Our relationship was going downhill by the day. Life was a living hell every single day. Amidst the doom and gloom, I realised that up to that point, my negative attitude was the cause of most of my bad experiences. Where did this negativity come from? As I introspected, I realised that I had been greatly influenced by my mother, who was a strong, authoritative and negative person at home.

When I was back in Malaysia, I realised that I had lost all the material things that I had chased after. I had lost my husband, the semi-detached house, the new Citroen car, and my job in the UK. I had also lost all my savings to an unworthy man, my dignity, my courage and my confidence. Gone too was my belief in Buddhism, which I had practised for more than 20 years. What I had gained was a daily living hell. I could only console myself that I still had my PhD qualification that later got me a senior lecturer position in SEGi University College. Most importantly, I had Nina with me and the baby in my womb. However, I could not imagine how to raise two young children on my own. It was beyond my strength. It was too difficult!

Chapter 2

A Precious Jasper

Newborn Boy

Zhen Kan, a precious jasper, was born in the early hours of November 18, 2011, at 1:08 a.m. I was all alone in the hospital without a husband, without a family member, without a friend because I was too ashamed to get in touch with any friend. Zhen Kan bore my surname, Chow. In Chinese, his name is 周正康, which means normal and healthy. I named him so because I was very worried that he would suffer the effects of the traumatic divorce I went through in Brazil during the pregnancy. Before he was born, the ultrasound scan had shown a double-loop umbilical cord entanglement around his neck. I even had a fall in the bathroom, but he survived in my womb. Zhen Kan was delivered via a Caesarean surgery due to the risk of the position of the umbilical cord and his reduced heartbeat during the labour. When the gynecologist took him out from my womb, I was relieved when I heard his first cry. I wanted to see him but the doctor sedated me to sleep immediately. It was the loneliest moment of my life, without a family member there to bring my baby to me after his birth.

As soon as I woke up the next morning, I asked for my baby. Tears rolled down my cheek at the sight of my beautiful baby boy. He was 3.53kg, healthy and normal. Zhen Kan had been in me throughout the toughest battle in Brazil and Malaysia and now, here he was. He looked very much like his older sister when she was born two years ago. My heart ached when days later, I registered his birth certificate without a father's name. *"I am sorry Zhen Kan... Mama is so sorry, please forgive me..."*

As I had to work full-time, I sent Nina to GCC kindergarten when she was 2 years old and hired a Filipina maid to take care of Zhen Kan at home. I always felt guilty for not spending time with my precious children, even at night because I was too tired. In addition, I had to wake up at least twice a night to breastfeed Zhen Kan.

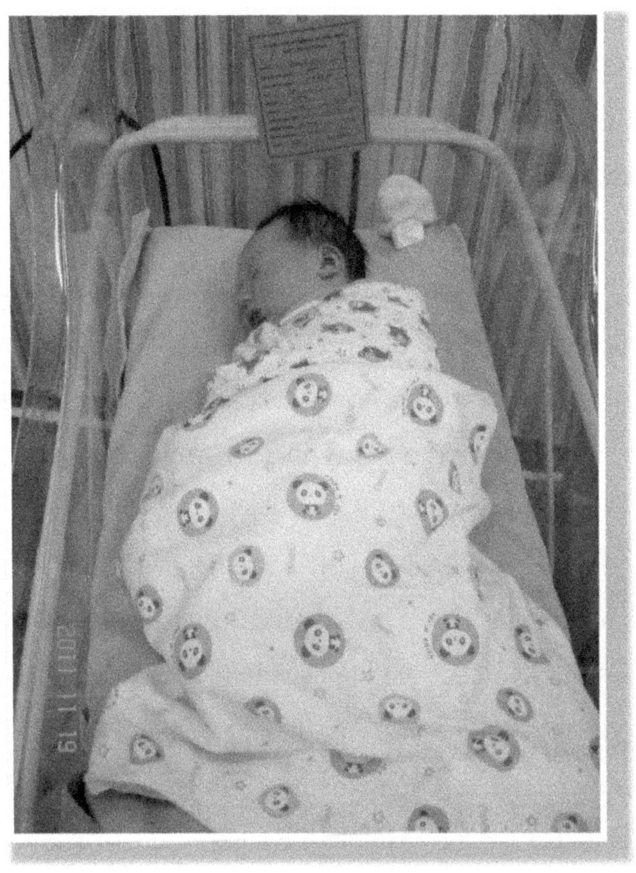

Newborn Zhen Kan – November 18, 2011.

Zhen Kan grew very well and was such a happy and delightful baby. My parents loved him a lot because he looked like me and his character was very similar to mine. Despite the blessing of a new grandchild, my parents continued to quarrel every day – between themselves, with my brother and with me. We were often shouting at one another. There was no peace at home. Of course, my children were affected. Nina continued to be grumpy, always screaming, crying and demanding her way. I was lost, very confused and had no idea how to teach Nina. My parents also fought over the maid and my mother accused my father of having an affair with her.

During a parent-teacher meeting in GCC, I met the principal, Jennie Seet. She suspected that Nina was autistic because she avoided eye contact with teachers and did not speak much. When I told her about my family problems, I broke down. Her reaction was unusual as she came close to me and embraced me. Although we had just met for the first time, I felt that she cared for me and wanted very much to help me. She offered to accept both my children in her childcare centre at a discounted rate. Since I was very upset with my parents and the maid, I sent the maid back to the Philippines without a second thought and put Nina and Zhen Kan in GCC childcare centre. But later, I realised that it was not a wise decision. After the maid left, I had to do all the housework, look after two children at night, plus wake up at midnight to feed Zhen Kan in addition to working full time in the day. I became even grumpier, more tired and angry with everyone around me. I had no rest and plunged deeper into my living hell.

13-month-old Zhen Kan and 3-year-old Nina.

Zhen Kan's Illness

Zhen Kan was only 18 months old when I put him in GCC childcare centre. He often suffered from colds that lasted several weeks despite medication. One day at the end of June 2013 after two months in GCC, the teacher phoned me to take him to the doctor because there were red rashes on his body. I took him to two clinics but they did not give him any antibiotics although his temperature continued to rise. I was so grumpy and tired with the housework and a sick child. One night, after cleaning him up from soiling his diaper, I noticed he was pale and restless. I took him downstairs and held him close to my chest. Suddenly, he cried out loud *"Mama"* and had a fit! He fell unconscious! I was shocked and was terrified that he would die. Immediately, we (my parents, Nina and I) took him to the nearest hospital, the Columbia Hospital. In the car, I heard him breathing again. In the hospital, he woke up and called, *"Mama, Po Po (grandma), Gong Gong (grandpa), Nini (Nina)."* We were relieved for a short while. The nurse said his temperature was very high, at 41°C. To reduce it quickly, they gave him a cold shower. My heart broke when I saw him shivering in the icy cold water. *"Mama feels so sorry for you, Zhen Kan..."* I wished I could take his place. Somehow, at that moment, I decided to stop being angry and quarrelling with my parents. Zhen Kan stayed in the hospital for four days but did not show signs of recovery. His abdomen became very bloated and on the third day, I noticed the edge of his eyes was turning yellow. However, the doctor discharged him when his fever subsided. Back home that night, Zhen Kan couldn't sleep well. He was breathless and his fever returned. When I brought him back to Columbia Hospital, the doctor recommended him to the University Malaya Medical Centre (UMMC) due to complications in his liver.

Zhen Kan stayed at UMMC for three weeks. I was with him round the clock. I informed GCC childcare centre principal Jennie Seet about his ailment and asked for a refund of the advanced fees that I had paid for the next few months because I would not be sending him there after his discharge. She agreed to my request. Beyond my expectation, Jennie, her husband (Alex) and 2 GCC teachers (Esther and Stephanie) came to visit us in the hospital that same night. They were practically strangers to me and yet, they came to visit us in the hospital. I was touched as I had not met such caring and compassionate people in my life before. They prayed for Zhen Kan and I don't remember exactly what they prayed except the last words, *"in Jesus' name"*! After their prayer, I felt a cool breeze brushing me and dismissed it as the wind from the air-conditioner. Now I believe that it was the Holy Spirit's work! After this, two colleagues from SEGi, Alex and Anthony, visited us; they were also Christians. Then, another colleague, Yit Wei, brought her cell group members to visit and pray for us. I wondered why Christians were so caring and loving.

The doctors were not able to diagnose the source of his fever and liver problems. Eventually, they treated him as atypical Kawasaki and gave him IVIG. During this period, Jennie also asked Pastor Francis Ho and his wife, Christine, from Christ Lutheran Church to visit and pray for us. Jennie also visited us a few times and brought some toys for Zhen Kan. She started to teach me to pray in Jesus' name. I still believed in Buddhism then, so I was praying to both since I wasn't sure which one was better.

Zhen Kan was discharged after three weeks when his fever subsided. However, his skin was still yellowish. This was the longest stay in hospital in my life and his life. During this time, Nina stayed with my mother and she grew very thin. We missed each other so much. When I brought Zhen Kan back to UMMC for his checkup, his jaundice condition persisted. The doctor decided to call him back to UMMC in August 2013 to do a liver biopsy for further investigation. However, they still could not find anything through the biopsy. I have a "never give up" spirit, so I searched online and found the best pediatric hepatic doctor in Malaysia – Dr Lim Chooi Bee from Selayang Hospital. I decided to transfer Zhen Kan there. When I informed Principal Jennie, she and her husband drove to my house the night before the admission. We had a long chat in her car. I asked her, *"Why have so many bad things happened to me? Why do I suffer so much? Will God heal my son?"* Her reply was intriguing. She said there was a very powerful angel in heaven who was the head of angels, but he did not obey God. Therefore, God cast him down to earth. He was Satan, who created havoc on earth, heaping all kinds of suffering on people. When we were in Selayang Hospital, Jennie also came to visit and pray for us. The GCC teachers, Esther and Stephenie, also visited us.

When I met Dr Lim in Selayang Hospital, she was impressed with my eagerness to bring my son to see her even before the reference letter from UMMC arrived. She told me, *"I'm not God, I cannot heal everyone. I will do my job."* The diagnosis process involved many blood and urine tests. In order to check for Wilson disease, the doctor inserted a tube into Zhen Kan's urethra to collect a complete urine sample over 48 hours for two sessions. I was not allowed in the room during the medical procedure. Zhen Kan wailed in pain.

When the procedure was over, Zhen Kan had difficulty passing urine, and his penis looked "bent"! It was so heart-wrenching to see this! I could have sued the medical officer for being so rough with him. Dr Lim diagnosed Zhen Kan as suffering from Alagille syndrome, a hereditary issue from the parents. She suspected that it was from my side of the family but nobody in my family, including me, had any liver disorder. Dr Lim told me to thank God that I was healthy although I might carry the gene. However, the genetic DNA test on Zhen Kan in Hospital Kuala Lumpur showed a negative result for the *zag-1* gene. Dr Lim told me about the risk of liver transplants, and the difficulty of finding the best-match liver and donor. My blood type is A, but Zhen Kan's was O. Dr Lim was upfront about all the disadvantages of liver transplant, warning me that the post-transplant life would be very difficult for Zhen Kan and me. He would need to take 15 drugs for the rest of his life and be admitted to the hospital very frequently, which would affect my job and Nina. Furthermore, the lifespan of liver transplant patients is not long, perhaps less than 10 years. It is a major surgery with a very high risk and complication and would overwhelm Zhen Kan for the rest of his life. Dr Lim was very sympathetic when she learned of my situation – the only bread winner with a 3-year-old daughter. I could not afford to stay in hospital for too long, therefore she did not recommend a liver transplant for Zhen Kan. I then asked God for a miraculous healing for Zhen Kan by giving him a new liver. When Dr Lim met Nina in the hospital, she saw the abnormality in Nina's behaviour and referred her to a child psychiatrist in Selayang Hospital. My plate of troubles was spilling over. How much more could I take? First, Zhen Kan. Then, Nina. Sorrow upon sorrow. A broken life plus a broken heart.

Seeking Healing

A mother's love is limitless, and I would do anything, pay any price, try anything for Zhen Kan's full recovery. I brought Zhen Kan to many hospitals and tried various alternative medicines. I also brought him to see pediatricians in Gleneagles Hospital, Pantai Hospital, and Tawakal Hospital. After consulting all the Western doctors, they all concluded that it all depended on Zhen Kan's constitution, and that Selayang Hospital was the best hospital to treat liver patients. I did not give up. Many friends, relatives, colleagues and neighbours tried to help and recommended alternative treatments. My colleague introduced Indian herbal medicine from an Indian doctor. My father told me to try the herbal medicine prepared by my uncle in Ipoh, claiming that it had healed some adult liver patients. My neighbour brought us to a spiritual healer in Tanjung Karan for a "spiritual steam healing" session, but he turned out to be a Malay "bomoh" (traditional medicine practitioner). My cousin brought us to Seremban for an underground water shower for detoxification and natural healing. Another friend told us to try the hot spring shower in Setapak Air Panas. And another friend introduced Chinese acupuncture by one Dr Liu. I tried all these and moved from one treatment to another but nothing worked. I tried a wild herb which had cured my father's Hepatitis B ailment. I also tried wild lotus, goat milk, liver tonic, Purtier Stem Cells and castor oil detox – all introduced by well-meaning friends and relatives.

Besides all these alternative medicine practices, I attempted all kinds of spiritual practices recommended by friends. It was a very confusing time. My colleague told me about the Buddhist God in Tian Hou Temple and encouraged me to bring my son there for prayers. But nothing happened. Then, I met someone at a hot spring shower who introduced me to a "Monkey God" in a Buddhist temple. I brought my son there for prayers and gave offerings, took their "yellow paper" home to boil and drink. Again, nothing happened and I didn't feel good about participating in all these practices.

Meanwhile, I chanted the Buddhist Daimoku and prayed in Jesus' name. Principal Jennie also brought Pastor Francis, Pastor Eric and Christine to visit us at home and pray for us. When they started to pray in tongues, I was not alarmed; instead, I was comforted. I naturally opened my heart to them and shared everything that was happening to Zhen Kan. When some Buddhist friends visited us, I found it hard to open my heart to them and therefore, spoke little. My Christian colleague, Yit Wei, also brought her cell group members to visit us and pray for us. Once again, I readily opened my heart to them and cried as I shared my painful ordeal with them.

It was not easy to care for Zhen Kan, having to work full time and look after the demanding Nina. The jaundice on Zhen Kan caused severe itch on his body and he scratched his skin day and night. At night, he would wake up several times for his feed. After drinking his milk, he would not be able to sleep and would keep scratching his skin. I was exhausted, badly deprived of sleep, yet believing that Zhen Kan would be healed one day.

My parents continued to argue a lot at home. Anguish continued to engulf the home and their quarrels exacerbated my stress. Once, my mother was so angry with my father that she took out a big chopper to threaten him. There was absolutely no peace at home. Indeed, there was a very strong spiritual warfare in this home. Finally, I mustered all my courage to move out from my parents' house. In January 2014, I moved into a rented apartment very close to the hill with my two children and a new Indonesian maid, hoping that the fresh air would help with my son's recovery. As soon as I moved out, my heart was filled with an unprecedented peace. No more distressing sounds of fighting, complaining and arguing.

Leap of Faith

One day, I bumped into Principal Jennie in GCC childcare centre when I was picking up Nina. She shared the testimony of her friend who had died from cancer but had no fear at all because she had Jesus with her. After her friend passed away, Jennie dreamed she was in heaven. She looked very happy, had long beautiful hair and wore a white long robe. Coincidentally, her sister saw the exact same picture. I had never heard any story like this before and was very curious to know more about Jesus and heaven. Jennie invited me to Christ Lutheran Church on the following Sunday. I agreed and since I had already moved out from my parents' home, I didn't need to tell them and get their approval. My mother was a staunch Buddhist and would have objected to me going to church.

On January 26, 2014, I walked into church for the first time in my life to seek Jesus and healing for my son. Nina and Zhen Kan were with me. I was shocked at the loud worship music because I was expecting soft, soothing songs. One of the songs was *Divine Exchange*, which was sung again during the prayer before the service ended. Pastor Eric Mau gave the sermon that morning. Zhen Kan's body itched so badly throughout the service that he had to take off his shirt to scratch his body. Pastor Eric prayed for him. However, he had a fever the next day and had to be admitted to Selayang Hospital. I did not understand this kind of reverse effect from seeking Jesus. Jennie explained that it was the work of Satan, who always tries to stop people from believing Jesus. I believed her and continued to pray in Jesus' name.

Pastor Francis, Christine, and Jennie visited us in Selayang Hospital, together with another couple, Simon and Anne who sat behind us during our first church service. Pastor Francis told me to surrender my son to God. "*How?*" I asked him. He replied, "*Let him be baptised.*" I agreed and immediately, Pastor Francis and Jennie baptised him in the hospital. It was only then that I knew that Jennie was also a pastor. No wonder she had been so loving and caring. I asked her to be Zhen Kan's godmother because I had never known anybody who cared for my son the way she did. As they prayed for us in tongues, I asked them to teach me. Pastor Jennie prayed for me to receive the gift of praying in tongues. Christine told me, *"There is no need to do the Buddhism chant anymore, just pray in Jesus' name and in tongues."* I was still doubtful. Before they left, Anne shared her testimony with me. Her family used to practise the same Buddhism as mine but nothing good happened until they believed in Jesus. Many good things and blessings then flowed into their life. Amazingly, God had sent the right person to me at the right moment. After several divine encounters with Christians plus one simple, yet closely related testimony, I decided to give up Buddhism because I had not received many blessings in my life all this while. When Anne told me the commandment of *"only worship one God"*, who is the Lord Jesus, I decided to pray in Jesus' name only and surrendered my Buddhist altar and scroll to Pastor Francis.

Zhen Kan and his godmother, Pastor Jennie,
in Selayang Hospital.

After Zhen Kan was discharged, I brought him and Nina to church every Sunday without fail. A friend in church, Susan, gave me a NIV Bible. I started reading it and found it to be the most interesting book I had ever read in my life, even though it was an older version from 1984. I used to read the Buddhism books and found that it didn't make sense. But when I read the Holy Bible, I wanted to read more and more. Eager and hungry to know who Jesus and God was, and how to get healing for my son, I memorised Bible verses for healing and every day, I prayed several Scripture verses, inserting Zhen Kan's name into them:

Surely Jesus took up our infirmities and carried our sorrows, yet we considered him stricken by God, smitten by him, and afflicted. But he was pierced for Zhen Kan's transgressions, he was crushed for Zhen Kan's iniquities; the punishment that brought Zhen Kan peace was upon him, and by his wounds Zhen Kan is healed. (Isaiah 53:4-5)

Zhen Kan will not die but live, and will proclaim what the Lord has done. (Psalm 118:17)

Jesus himself bore our sins in his body on the tree, so that Zhen Kan might die to sins and live for righteousness; by his wounds Zhen Kan have been healed. (1 Peter 2:24)

And if the Spirit of him who raised Jesus from the dead is living in Zhen Kan, he who raised Christ from the dead will also give life to Zhen Kan mortal bodies through his Spirit, who lives in Zhen Kan. (Romans 8:11)

Indeed, Zhen Kan was ill, and almost died. But God had mercy on him, and not on him only but also on me, to spare me sorrow upon sorrow. (Philippians 2:27)

Zhen Kan will grow and become strong; he is filled with wisdom and grace of God was upon him. (Luke 2:40)

Don't be afraid; just believe, and Zhen Kan will be healed. (Luke 8:50)

I also memorised Psalm 23 and read Psalm 91 over Zhen Kan every day. I surrendered Zhen Kan to God, pleading with God to heal him and use him to do His work when Zhen Kan grew up. Whenever Zhen Kan woke up in the middle of the night, after giving him milk and putting him back to sleep, I would kneel before God and repeatedly asked God to give him a new liver, confessing that "by *Jesus's stripes, Zhen Kan is healed!*" As written in the Bible, *"Whatever you ask for in prayer, believe that you have received it, and it will be yours.*" (Mark 11:24). I believed that Zhen Kan was healed and gave thanks to Jesus for healing him.

Often, I wondered if I had done anything wrong to cause Zhen Kan's severe sickness. Zhen Kan was innocent, too young to have done anything wrong to deserve all the pain and suffering. John 9:1-3 dispelled my doubts and encouraged me much: "*As he went along, he saw a man blind from birth. His disciples asked him, "Rabbi, who sinned, this man or his parents, that he was born blind?" "Neither this man nor his parents sinned," said Jesus, "but this happened so that the works of God might be displayed in him." *" This passage convinced me that God wanted to display His work and glory by healing Zhen Kan. We attended Sunday service without fail, except when we were in the hospital. Every Sunday when we went to church, I had great hope that Zhen Kan would be miraculously healed. Although there was no sign of healing and all the blood test results showed his liver deteriorating, I did not give up; I kept praying and hoping for a miracle. Pastor Francis and brother How Chai told me to forgive and let go of all my past bitterness, especially for Zhen Kan's father. I did exactly what they told me. Not only did I forgive my ex-husband and his parents, I also contacted them to inform them of Nina's well-being and Zhen Kan's sickness. When I left Brazil with Nina, I resolved to sever all ties with them but God has healed my heart and taught me to forgive.

Whenever there was a healing crusade or when a preacher renowned for the gift of healing came to town, I took Zhen Kan to the meeting. When I heard about the Healing Room in Glad Tidings church, I took him there for prayer every Monday night. I also attended my church's Friday prayer meeting. Battling Zhen Kan's illness was a long, exhausting journey and I felt very old and worn out. From March to June 2014, Zhen Kan was admitted to hospital every month due to fever and infection. Whenever we were in the hospital, Pastor Jennie and Pastor Francis came to pray for us. Besides them, God also sent another two faithful sisters from other churches to visit, encourage and pray for us. They were Ruth from the Healing Room and Vicky, whom I had met in the Christian Fellowship in SEGi University. When Pastor Jennie was not in Malaysia, Ruth and Vicky were my best soulmates who encouraged me and taught me a lot about Jesus. I was very touched by all the people that God sent into my life to give me "speedy" lessons about Him. God's grace was upon me because He had sustained me throughout this journey without me collapsing or falling ill. *"Thank you Jesus for Your grace upon me!"*

During our time in the hospital, I read pages and pages of the Bible every day. Once, God spoke to me through Psalm 27: 13-14: *"I am still confident of this: I will see the goodness of the Lord in the land of the living. Wait for the Lord; be strong and take heart and wait for the Lord."* Surely, God was going to heal my son so that I would see His goodness in the land of the living on earth, I thought! In fact, a few nights before admitting Zhen Kan to hospital, I saw him in my dream; he had grown up a bit, was wearing a white robe and looked completely healthy and fair. The usual yellowish tint on his skin was gone. In my dream, I saw someone carrying him away.

Zhen Kan always encouraged me by saying, in Mandarin, *"Ma, don't cry!"* If he saw his sister Nina crying, he would go to her and stroke her hair to comfort her. Occasionally, he cried but he would quickly dry his tears with his t-shirt! Once, he went up to a crying Nina and lifted his t-shirt to dry her tears! What an amazing child, taking care of his older sister when he himself was so sick! Whenever I was angry or grumpy, Zhen Kan would say in Mandarin, *"Ma, don't be angry. Ma, don't be grumpy."* He had a maturity beyond that of a 2-year-old boy, and beyond that of an innocent, sick child. The gracious hand of God was upon this precious child.

All the pain and exhaustion of caring for Zhen Kan did not hinder my career. I wanted to be a professor, to do research in my field of electrical engineering but there were not many opportunities for research in SEGi University. So, I applied to several government research universities. It was truly God's favour when I was offered a Senior Lecturer position at University of Malaya, the first and the top university in Malaysia. In fact, it is very hard for a Chinese to gain appointment in that university, but God gave me a new job to lift me up when I was so worn out from caring for my son. This was the first tangible blessing from God after I believed in Jesus. Although there was a slight pay cut, I believed that my career would progress at University of Malaya. A new challenge of research and career lay ahead of me.

A Bravc Little Boy

In June 2014, Zhen Kan was admitted to Selayang Hospital on the second day of my new job at University of Malaya. His condition was worsening and Dr Lim asked me to sign the consent form relating to his impending death. I still did not believe Dr Lim because I was convinced that

Jesus would heal Zhen Kan even right to the last moment, just like how He raised Lazarus from the dead. Dr Lim prescribed the two strongest antibiotics for Zhen Kan to resolve his infection. Both didn't work. His liver became very swollen, growing to 12cm instead of the normal 3cm for his age. Dr Lim said a liver patient at this final stage with such a swollen liver would feel enormous pain, but amazingly, Zhen Kan did not feel any pain. He barely cried in the hospital. He was very tired and slept most of the time. Every day and night, I was at his bedside, praying for him unceasingly and crying buckets. Zhen Kan would calmly say to me in Mandarin, "*Ma, don't cry.*" He was so collected and mature for his age even though he was going through all the unnecessary pain. Whenever he faced the syringe, he would not cry but just clenched his teeth and endured the pain without dropping a tear! What a brave 2-year-old boy! My heart broke and I wept when I saw all the needles sticking on his body. The doctors and nurses were always very impressed with him and would say, "*You are such a good boy!*" In the ward, the children on the other beds would normally cry but not Zhen Kan. He would just sleep, look at me, or listen to me quietly. God was gracious to allow Zhen Kan to suffer the illness but not the pain. I learned a very simple but beautiful children's song, and would sing to Zhen Kan in the hospital,

"Jesus loves me this I know, for the Bible tells me so. Little one to Him belong, they are weak but he is strong. Yes Jesus loves me, Yes Jesus loves me, Yes Jesus loves me, the Bible tells me so."

One morning, when I was in the toilet in the hospital, I heard a voice, *"Zhen Kan does not belong to me, he belongs to God."* A great relief flooded my heart; it was not for me to worry about his life and death because he belonged to God. God would look after him, whether in heaven or on earth. When I told Pastor Jennie about what I heard, I felt the shivers from the top of my head to the bottom of my feet. She said the message was indeed from God as she had heard similar testimonies before. I wondered why God spoke to me in the toilet – not the cleanest place to be in the government hospital. Later, I understood that God came into my life and spoke to me in my darkest hours because He really loved me and wanted to save me. That was the first time I heard from God personally. It was not an audible voice, but a very subtle, assuring and comforting voice. Pastor Jennie also told me to prepare myself, because in her prayers, she always saw Zhen Kan with Jesus. I saw Pastor Jennie whispering into his ear; maybe it was a prayer or a message. She also told me to prepare Zhen Kan for heaven and assured him that Jesus loved him and I would be with him one day. This time, however, I did not believe what she said. I was still convinced that Jesus would heal Zhen Kan. Nevertheless, I took her advice. I told Zhen Kan, *"Zhen Kan, Mama loves you so much. Jesus also loves you very much. If Jesus comes, hold His hand. He will take you to heaven. Mama will come soon."* After telling Zhen Kan this, I couldn't believe that I had said it. Had I given up?

After three weeks in the hospital, Zhen Kan miraculously recovered from the infection, not through the medicine but by the power of God. When his fever subsided, Dr Lim discharged him immediately. Hallelujah! Zhen Kan was still alive and we returned home! This time, I really believed that Jesus would heal Zhen Kan even after Dr Lim had pronounced his imminent death. We had proven her wrong! I continued to pray earnestly day and night for his healing. When Zhen Kan had high grade fever again, I did not take him to the hospital anymore because I felt the antibiotics had not healed him but had worsened his condition instead. I prayed Isaiah 53:5 over him, *"By Jesus' stripes, Zhen Kan is healed!"* Day and night, I used this verse to claim healing for Zhen Kan. Miraculously, Zhen Kan recovered from the high fever of 39^{0}C overnight, even without the antibiotics. This assured me that Jesus was with us and He would heal Zhen Kan. In my quiet moments when

I reflected on all that had happened, I would be overwhelmed with gratitude to God. When I first returned to Malaysia, I thought I had plunged deeper into the living hell, but my situation then (with Zhen Kan's sickness) was even worse. I had come to know Jesus on whom I could put my hope and trust for Zhen Kan's healing and a better future for us.

The stress of caring for Zhen Kan and Nina, and my full-time job greatly affected my moods. I was grumpy, waking up several times at night when Zhen Kan woke up to drink milk, passed motion and scratched himself. I had to tenderly wipe his itchy skin with a damp cloth to soothe him to sleep before I could return to sleep. But in an hour's time, all these would repeat and I had to wake up to take care of him again. For more than a year from the time Zhen Kan fell ill, I was severely deprived of sleep. In fact, I had been suffering sleep deprivation since Nina was born because I breastfed both of them. That means that I had not had a good night's sleep for more than four years. One night, Zhen Kan said (in Mandarin), "*Ma, don't cry. Ma, don't be angry. Ma, don't be grumpy*". I was very touched by his maturity and understanding even though he was only 2 years old and was so sick! Zhen Kan often comforted me and Nina by stroking our hair. *You are my beloved precious jasper! You are an angel to us!*

Zhen Kan holding God's medical prayer booklet,
given by Pastor Jennie.

Chapter 3

Journey to Heaven

Reunion

My former parents-in-law from Brazil missed Nina very much and they wanted to visit us in Malaysia to see Nina and Zhen Kan. I had been soaking myself so much in prayer for Zhen Kan's healing that I had completely forgotten their cruel treatment of me in Brazil. I welcomed them to Malaysia with open arms and let them stay in my apartment so that they could spend some quality time with their grandchildren. They were taken aback by my hospitality because they had once chased me out of their apartment in Brazil. I had learned from the Bible in Romans 12:17-21:

Do not repay anyone evil by evil. Be careful to do what is right in the eyes of everybody. If it is possible, as far as it depends on you, live at peace with everyone. Do not take revenge, my friends, but leave room for God's wrath, for it is written: "It is mine to avenge; I will repay." On the contrary: "If your enemy is hungry, feed him; If he is thirsty, give him something to drink. In doing this, you will heap burning coals on his head." Do not overcome by evil, but overcome evil with good.

I knew they missed their grandchildren and longed to see them. So, I allowed them to do so, even letting them stay in my apartment and enjoy the precious time with their grandchildren. How amazing God's grace is – He helped me to forgive and also forget my bitter experience in Brazil.

My former parents-in-law could not speak English, so they brought along their niece, Beatriz – an English teacher. I did not do anything special for them as I was very busy working full time in the day and looking after Zhen Kan and Nina at night. Surprisingly, God vindicated me during their stay in Malaysia. My former parents-in-law apologised to me for having misunderstood me and believing all the lies their son had told them about me. My former mother-in-law said to me, *"You are the best mother caring for the children, you look after both children very well, and are very patient, the most hardworking mother, a beautiful and intelligent woman.*" It was the best compliment I had ever received from her since I married her son. They knew how difficult it was to raise and teach Nina, whose character was very similar to their son, who had given them a hard time all their life until then! On top of that, they saw how difficult it was to take care of a sick child, all on my own without a husband. Finally, they realised that their son was wrong. I felt that God had given me justice even though I had not asked for it.

Return to Brazil

After knowing Zhen Kan's liver condition, they offered to take Zhen Kan to Brazil for a liver transplant. I thought it was not possible and not a good solution as Dr Lim had told me about all the disadvantages of a liver transplant. But she had mentioned that Brazil had a very good liver transplant programme. I sought her advice and she said it would be too late for Zhen Kan to do the liver transplant because his body was too weak and he might have internal bleeding anytime. Furthermore, the high pressure on the plane would deal a serious blow on his body. It was too risky and dangerous for Zhen Kan to travel more than 30 hours to Brazil. Nevertheless, I still had the "never give up" spirit and

I could not just stand and see my son die without trying. I thought – God had not healed Zhen Kan in Malaysia; was He going to heal him in Brazil, where he was conceived?

One day, a church member, Elaine, asked me to take Zhen Kan to an evangelistic prayer conference. We did and during the worship singing, my tears poured when they sang "*Yahweh...Yahweh...*" I did not understand why because I did not know the meaning of Yahweh at that time. Pastor Benedict Rajan shared a testimony about a paralysed child who was healed and could walk and talk. The parents were not Christians when they heard about Pastor Benedict. They just brought their son to him for prayer. I was desperate and asked if any church member could go with me to see Pastor Benedict personally. Brother Neo graciously drove us to Johor to seek his prayer. I asked Pastor Benedict whether Zhen Kan should go for the liver transplant, whether in Malaysia or Brazil. He said he needed to pray and ask God first. A few days later, he told me to let Zhen Kan have a liver transplant for his complete healing. *"Please go back to Brazil,"* he said. I told my former parents-in-law, and asked Beatriz to ask my ex-husband if he was willing to donate part of his liver to his son. They both have the same blood type, "O", whereas mine is "A". I was very relieved when Mr. L agreed. He had denied his son when Zhen Kan was in my womb. I thought it would be a great opportunity for him to do something for his son so that I could tell Zhen Kan in future that his father loved him although the marriage did not work out. Again, Dr Lim said that Zhen Kan was too weak to fly and undergo the liver transplant. It would be at our own risk, but I trusted that the message from Pastor Benedict was from God.

On August 20, 2014 (Wednesday), I made the decision to go to Brazil for the liver transplant. By then, Zhen Kan was critically ill and his life was hanging by a thread. Without further delay, we bought the flight tickets to depart on August 25. It was a very long journey. Thankfully, we managed to fly with my former parents-in-law. That was a great help. Besides Zhen Kan and Nina, my Indonesian maid, Maria, came along. Technically, I only had two days to sort out three travel documents: apply for a passport for Zhen Kan, renew the Dependent Visa for Nina at the Immigration office, and apply for a tourist visa for Maria at the Brazilian Embassy. These were seemingly impossible tasks, considering that I was dealing with the Immigration department and the embassy at the very last minute. I told God that if it was His will to bring Zhen Kan to Brazil, then help me to get the documents sorted out by Friday so that we could fly on Monday. He did! All were done Friday, late afternoon. My former parents-in-law were overjoyed with my decision to bring Zhen Kan to Brazil as they really wanted to do something for Zhen Kan. They paid for all our flight tickets, made all the arrangements for us, and got in touch with the surgeon in Brazil.

We departed on August 25 at 2:00 a.m. to begin a total of three flights – 7 hours to Dubai, 14 hours to Rio de Janeiro, 2 hours to Porte Alegre (south of Brazil), and another 4 hours' car ride to Criciúma, the home of my former parents-in-law. In Dubai, we stayed for 2 nights while in transit. Zhen Kan was very tired from this long journey. When we were waiting at a hotel restaurant, he lay his head on a travel pillow on a table and slept quietly. Amazing child! This picture of him sleeping peacefully without any fuss, although he was extremely ill and exhausted, is imprinted deeply in my memory. In the hotel room, I ordered spaghetti bolognaise for my children. Zhen Kan and Nina ate a lot and very happily too. Little did I know that this was going to be the last meal for Zhen Kan on earth and the last meal for the three of us together! After 2 nights in Dubai, we took the next flight to Rio de Janeiro. We arrived in Brazil on August 27, 2014. When I checked my old passport, I realised that it was exactly the same day (August 27) three years ago when I left Brazil with Nina and Zhen Kan in my womb. It must be God's plan to bring us back here, I thought.

My former parents-in-law took an earlier connecting flight to Porte Alegre but we got a later flight due to late booking. We were all very tired and the jetlag was bad. Furthermore, Brazil's time zone is opposite that of Malaysia's. Nina was crying a lot and was very demanding. Suddenly, she had a fit! I was petrified and prayed immediately. Luckily, the fit lasted a few seconds and she was normal again. We endured our fatigue and waited for the next flight. Finally, we arrived in Criciúma at dawn on August 28, 2014. Thank God that we arrived safely, especially Zhen Kan who seemed to be fine throughout the journey without suffering from any bleeding. He just slept a lot. It was winter in Brazil and Zhen Kan felt very cold all the time. At night, his ear and nose bled a bit. We stayed at his grandparents' home. Zhen Kan had no appetite, just drank milk and slept. He asked me to sleep with him and hold his little hand. I did exactly what he asked. The next morning, I gave Zhen Kan a bath in a baby bathtub. He was happy and paddled in the water, saying, "*Swim...swim...*" That was the last time I bathed him. I wished it wasn't!

The next morning, my former father-in-law brought us to Hospital Pequeno Infantil in Curitiba, where Beatriz had contacted the surgeon for the liver transplant. I was very disappointed to find out that Mr. L had changed his mind about donating part of his liver. Not only that, he did not even come to see his own son at his parents' home or at the hospital. I felt cheated by my former parents-in-law. Since we were already in Brazil, I hoped to find a donor for Zhen Kan. Earlier, on the way to the hospital, my former father-in-law drove very fast on the highway. I was very worried, praying that there would be no car accident nor bleeding in Zhen Kan. When we stopped at a service station, Nina got a pink heart-shaped ice-cream, but Zhen Kan knew he could not eat and did not ask for one. Instead, he asked for a yellow heart-shaped candy. I agreed but I told him I would give it to him when he was well. Throughout the car journey, Zhen Kan lay on my lap. I felt very sad and lost and cried. Immediately, Zhen Kan noticed. He looked closely at me, feeling his mama's sadness. He wiped my nose with his clothes and stroked my hair to comfort me. My little Zhen Kan always touched my heart. He was always very caring and loving.

When we arrived in Curitiba, my former father-in-law took Nina and Maria to stay with a relative there. My heart was very heavy when I left their house because I did not know when we would return to see Nina. I was very worried about Nina because she was very agitated. Brazilians couldn't understand her as she spoke English, and Maria couldn't understand Portuguese. I had to harden my heart and quickly leave while Nina was crying. When we arrived at the hospital, Zhen Kan told me that he did not want to see a doctor. Zhen Kan knew that the doctor would poke needles into his hand for the drip and medicine; he had enough already! When the doctor examined Zhen Kan, Zhen Kan pretended that his hands hurt and hid them behind his back. Dr. Sylvio examined him but I was very disappointed that he did nothing for Zhen Kan that night although I told him that Zhen Kan's ear and nose were bleeding. He told me to continue with the previous medication and would do the blood tests the next morning.

We were put in the same room with two other children with liver disorder. There was a one-year-old boy who had a liver transplant a few months ago and had returned to the hospital due to infection. His mother told me that he had to be admitted to hospital frequently after the liver transplant. It was exactly what Dr. Lim told me in Selayang Hospital. The other patient was a 9-year-old girl, whose skin was very yellow and who looked very sad. She had her transplant with part of her mother's liver when she was a baby. Now, she was waiting for her second liver transplant!

There was no smile or childlike joy in her face. I felt very scared and I could not imagine what life would be like for Zhen Kan if he had a liver transplant. I did not want him to suffer like them. I just wanted a miraculous healing from God. That's why I had brought him to Brazil. I was too tired to pray and I could not think properly. I said to Jesus, *"Please take Zhen Kan home, or heal him now!"*

The Last Breath

During the first night in the hospital on August 29, 2014, Zhen Kan woke up a few times to pass motion and urine, and asked me to soothe his itchy skin. Around 11.20 p.m., Zhen Kan woke up again to pass motion in the toilet and scratched his skin. His nose was bleeding and I called the nurse many times to get the doctor. Finally, the doctor came but he just took a photo of Zhen Kan and told him to lie down. He said they would do something the next day. It was ridiculous! I could only tell Zhen Kan to sleep because I was terribly tired and exhausted. We both fell asleep in the dark room. Suddenly, Zhen Kan called out loudly, *"Mama!"* I woke up immediately and felt a strange and intense energy around us. Zhen Kan was already sitting up and asked me to hold him. I grabbed him and stood up. I felt a strange energy pulling him away from me. He was slightly lifted up and I heard a very unusual breathing sound coming from him… It was his LAST BREATH! But I didn't know it then!

I knew something was not right and turned on the light. His arm flopped from my shoulders! I yelled, *"Zhen Kan! Zhen Kan! Zhen Kan!!!"* many times but he did not respond. I shouted for the nurse and they rushed him to the emergency room. The doctor on call said that his breathing was slowing down and gave him an injection to relieve his pain. I tried to open his eyes to check his pupil, the way Dr Lim inspected him before. I noticed that the size of his pupil did not change with the light and there was no movement at all. OH MY!!! That was the end!!! I couldn't believe that it happened in Brazil after we had travelled half the world with our last hope! I was alone and terribly devastated in a foreign hospital without a friend. No hugs, no comfort from anybody, nobody…

The nurse told me to wait outside as they needed to resuscitate him. I walked out to a small church that I had seen earlier in the day. There was a statue of Jesus and Mary. I did not know it was a Roman Catholic Church. I knelt before the statue. I was a new Christian and knew nothing about the different Christian denominations. I just knelt down, badly torn and broken, streams of tears running down my cheeks. I cried, "*Jesus, please take Zhen Kan to heaven… and take me to visit him in heaven… I have lost everything in my life… this is the most painful one… I have nothing worth living…*" I had lost everything that I had chased in this world. No words can describe the pain of losing my beloved son. I could not kill myself although I did not wish to live; I knew I had to live because my 5-year-old daughter needed me. I continued to pray, "*Jesus, I do not wish to live for myself anymore, **I give my life to you, Jesus**. I will not chase anything for myself… I will do whatever you tell me to do…*" That was the *aha* moment when I gave my life to Jesus at 37 years old, when I realised that God is the Sovereign God who has control over the birth and death of all men. Nobody can do anything to change this. I was in fear of God, recognising Him as the God of the whole universe. I dared not leave Him although I did not love Him yet, as Christians would usually say.

I knew it was the end of Zhen Kan's life on earth. He was critically ill and the doctors were reluctant to do anything even though we had travelled from the other half of the world. I had hoped for a miracle when we arrived Brazil, an open heaven as a lady told me before, but I did not know whether it was true. I thought if I brought my son back to

Brazil to sort out the family grudges and misunderstanding, then miracles might happen in Brazil and Zhen Kan could be healed miraculously. Instead of reconciliation and healing, I met disappointment.

After a short while, the nurses brought Zhen Kan to the ICU, but I had to wait outside. I was crying alone outside the ICU room, sitting alone on a chair in front of a lift. Although it was midnight, people were coming in and out of the lift and watching me cry alone. I knew Zhen Kan was leaving… After a while, a nurse came to deliver the bad news. I went into the ICU room to see Zhen Kan. His abdomen was swollen, his body was lifeless but he was still the most beautiful son that I had ever had, the only one… that Mama loved so much… I opened his nappy and looked at his black stool for the last time… *"I'm sorry Zhen Kan, Mama can't clean you anymore. Since you were born, Mama has never slept well at night, waking up several times every night to breastfeed you. When you were sick, I looked after you day and night, night and day… I wiped and soothed you to sleep. I don't need to do this anymore because you have left me. I love you Zhen Kan! Mama will miss you, I wish to go with you, but I can't because I still need to raise your sister Nina who needs me very much…"*

Zhen Kan was born on November 18, 2011 at about 1:00 a.m. and he left me on August 30, 2014 at about 1:00 a.m. Only a very short period of 2 years and 9 months but he is forever in my heart, my angel who has led me to Jesus. No words can describe the pain of losing my beloved son, who had always encouraged me, saying, *"Ma, don't cry."* It was devastating after a long battle of persevering, never giving up hope and waiting for God to heal Zhen Kan. At least, I still witness the grace of God because He did not take away Zhen Kan while we were sleeping or while he was in the operation theatre. Instead, God woke him up and we had a last hug. Zhen Kan did not cry… no pain, no tear, no fear… just a goodbye hug for his mama before his last breath. I am still grateful to Jesus because I was with Zhen Kan at the very last moment of his earthly life! How many people get to be with their loved ones when they pass on or have a chance to say goodbye? Zhen Kan is enjoying a much better life now in heaven. No more hospital, no more needles, no more medicine, no more blood tests, no more pain, no more itch, no more sleepless nights... but a *Divine Exchange* with heaven for eternity and good health! That was the song – *Divine Exchange* – that we heard when we first walked into Christ Lutheran Church in January 2014.

Farewell

I lay on the sofa, waiting for the death report. I wept, sobbed and wailed, wondering why God had taken Zhen Kan home to heaven when we had travelled all the way to Brazil. Wouldn't it have been easier to take him home when we were in Malaysia? If I buried Zhen Kan in Brazil, I wouldn't be able to visit his grave often. What was God's plan? I still had not fully understood yet.

During the car ride back to Criciúma from Curitiba, Nina asked me, *"We need to take Zhen Kan home. Where is Zhen Kan?"* I was in deep misery but I had to tell Nina, *"Jesus has taken Zhen Kan to His home in heaven."* Nina asked, *"Can we go there to see Zhen Kan?"* I replied, *"We can't, it's very high up there."* Nina asked, *"Can we fly there in an areophane?"* I said, *"We can't, it's higher than the clouds. Only when Jesus comes can He take us there."* Nina continued to ask, *"Is there any hospital there?"* I answered through my sobs, *"There is no hospital in heaven. The doctor in the hospital here can't heal Zhen Kan, so Jesus has to take him home to heal him. Now, Zhen Kan is already healed and he doesn't have fever or yellow skin anymore."* Nina was crying as I talked to her. She missed Zhen Kan and seemed to know that we would not see him anytime soon. She was only 5 years old.

My former parents-in-law felt very sorry and sad. They arranged everything and paid for the funeral. They kept Zhen Kan's body in their Berti family *capela* – a special burial house for their family members only. In other words, they had finally recognised Zhen Kan as their grandson, although his biological father did not even turn up for the funeral! Mr. L was a coward and irresponsible father! I often comforted myself with this thought – *"I'm unfortunate to have a bad husband for 4 years, but I'm very fortunate not to have a bad husband for another 40 years!"* Regardless, Zhen Kan's body lies with his great-grandparents and ancestors in Brazil.

When we were walking with his coffin to the *capela*, I recognised the scene in my dream! Zhen Kan's death and burial were destined to be in Brazil! He died, not because I did not pray enough, or I prayed the wrong prayer, or I did not do enough to save him; it was simply God's will. God is the author and finisher of Zhen Kan's life, and He had already told me that *"Zhen Kan belongs to Me."* Certainly, God could take Zhen Kan home when his mission on earth was completed! Zhen Kan's death was definitely not because God had not forgiven my sins. Jesus forgave me the moment I accepted Him and asked for His forgiveness! He had died for my sins and taken away all my punishment on the cross

2000 years ago! The death of Zhen Kan was neither a punishment for me nor him.

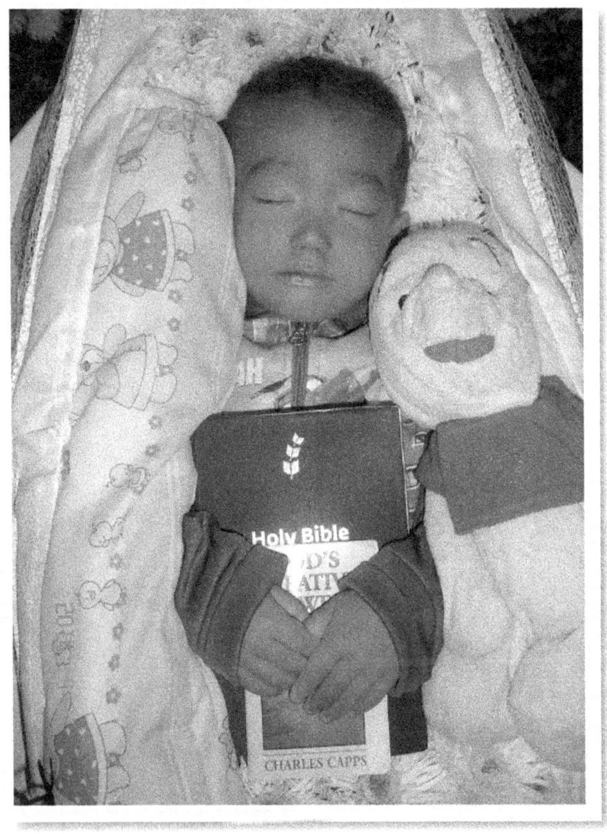

Zhen Kan was buried with the Holy Bible, God's medical prayer booklet, his favorite toy Winnie the Pooh, and his bolster.

Funeral of Zhen Kan in Brazil on August 31, 2014.

The capela of the Berti family where Zhen Kan's coffin was placed next to his great-grandfather's.

Battle to Go Home

After the funeral, I had to face another battle to take Nina back to Malaysia as she had a Brazilian passport. (Since our return to Malaysia in 2011, I had been applying for her to get the Malaysian citizenship, but to no avail.) According to the Brazilian law, there are only two ways to bring a child under 18 years old out of Brazil – (1) with the court's approval; or (2) with her father's approval. Nina's father was a liar from the start. He had reneged on his promise to donate his liver to Zhen Kan. During our divorce process, he lied to the judge in his attempt to get custody of Nina. Thank God that the court took my side. When I was pregnant and divorced, the court allowed me to take Nina out of Brazil back to Malaysia. But now, I had no valid reason to get the court's support. In any case, the court approval process could take a few months, with no certainty of success. The surest and fastest way was to get her father's consent. *Dear Lord Jesus, I really need your favour!*

Every morning, I prayed Psalm 27:1-3, which I had memorised in my heart. These verses spoke deeply to my heart:

The Lord is my light and my salvation – whom shall I fear? The Lord is the stronghold of my life – of whom shall I be afraid? When evil men advance against me to devour my flesh, when my enemies and my foes attack me, they will stumble and fall. Though an army besiege me, my heart will not fear; though war break out against me, even then will I be confident.

No matter how evil Mr. L was, I would not fear him. Three years ago, I had won the battle by my own might without faith in God. But now I have the Almighty God with me, so whom shall I fear? I was determined to get his consent to take Nina back to Malaysia.

My former parents-in-law were very upset with their son, who had given them a lot of troubles and heartaches. I had experienced their pain three years ago. Living with this man had been a nightmare. He was so violent that once, he nearly punched his mother's face. Fortunately, his sister was quick enough to restrain him. He had quarrelled with them and blamed his mother for all his problems. Yet, he was still asking his father for money. How ridiculous it was that a grown man like him still could not support himself! What an irresponsible spendthrift!

My former father-in-law tried communicating with his son about Nina's issue. Mr. L requested to take Nina to a party, without me. I had to relent and let him see his daughter as I needed his consent. When they returned, Nina was crying and agitated. He was not able to soothe her. I found out that Nina had been fighting with the other children in the restaurant while he was having dinner with his friend. He had no idea how to look after Nina and he did not understand her at all. The next day, my former father-in-law asked Mr. L and his girlfriend to join the family and relatives for lunch at their beach apartment. I was very surprised to see him. Even their relatives were incensed when they saw him because they did not like this heartless man too. As for me, I tried to be friendly with his girlfriend because I needed her to persuade him to give his consent. I looked up to the sky and prayed to God to give her many children to satisfy Mr. L so that he would not bother Nina in the future. After lunch, Beatriz and her husband decided to leave earlier, and took me and Nina along. When Mr. L discovered that we had left, he became raving mad and turned all the tables upside down, smashed a picture that he thought his aunt had given me, pulled out a bunch of grass from the ground and threw it at his mother's face! He was uncontrollable! No wonder his mother told me that he needed medication to stay calm. To appease him, my former parents-in-law quickly phoned us to return to the beach apartment. Mr. L kept on raging and accusing everyone of doing him wrong. I calmly said to him, *"Yes, we are all wrong, you are right!"* Then he calmed down. I was surprised at myself and thanked God for steadying my nerves. Had this happen three years ago, I would be fighting with him. Not anymore.

Mr. L then asked to take Nina away to the beach in another city with his girlfriend, again forbidding me to go along. He agreed to bring her back that night. He did not. Again, he lied. I kept on praying. Finally, he brought Nina back to me with the consent letter signed by him, allowing me to take Nina back to Malaysia. Praise the Lord! Soon, Nina and I were on our way home! This was the second time I took Nina away from Brazil, to the other half of the world. But this time, without Zhen Kan, neither in my womb nor by my side. I cried throughout the 30-hour plane ride but I felt stronger than the first time because I had Jesus with me in my life to direct my path, my way and my future!

Zhen Kan "Chow Berti" – Dignity and Justice

A few weeks later, I received some photos of Zhen Kan's memorial from my former mother-in-law. They had given Zhen Kan the surname "Chow Berti". This was significant because it meant that I had at last received "dignity" and "justice" for Zhen Kan and me. Three years ago, Mr. L had accused me of having an affair and rejected the baby in my womb. I returned to Malaysia pregnant, divorced and full of shame. Mr. L's rejection of his very own son had been extremely hurtful and I had not filled in the father's name in Zhen Kan's birth certificate. Finally, Zhen Kan's paternal family had acknowledged him as theirs, and given him the surname "Chow Berti", just like his older sister, Nina Chow Berti. The surname represents these two children's bloodline – the Chow and Berti families. Restoring Zhen Kan's dignity was the best gift that I could give him, because I dared to take him to Brazil before he died. I said to Zhen Kan in my heart, "*You have brought Mama dignity and justice even though you have left!*" Zhen Kan is such an amazing boy! *Thank you Jesus!*

Memorial of Zhen Kan Chow Berti.

*The surname "Chow Berti" that granted us
dignity and justice.*

Chapter 4

Grief & Bereavement

A Third Life

When we came back to Malaysia, I felt like I was starting a third life, with Nina as my reason for living. I was starting my new job at University of Malaya. By His grace, I still had the job even though I had taken two weeks' unpaid leave from the second day of my new employment. I had been badly tormented emotionally and physically, especially in the past three years since the divorce up to the point of my beloved son's death. I tried to comfort myself that finally, I could sleep through the night, no more caring for a sick child, no more hospital stays, and no hospital expenses to pay. I only needed to take care of one child, Nina. Such a comforting thought after such a harrowing ordeal.

However, my heart and my life had been broken into a million pieces all these years. There was much bitterness and anguish that needed to be resolved. I prayed for healing for my soul and restoration of my whole being. Without Jesus, I would not have any courage, confidence, and hope to live another day. Still, it was not easy dealing with the grief of losing my son. I understood then that God was the Creator of everything, He was the author of Zhen Kan's life. He decided his birth and death, his mission, his parents, his bloodline, his everything.... When Zhen Kan's mission was done, God took him home to heaven. For sure, Zhen Kan's mission was to lead me to Christ! Before knowing Jesus, I had been such a staunch Buddhist and vowed never to leave the Nichiren Buddhism. I was very certain that it was the only true religion. But now, I believed that God loved me so much that He could even turn ashes into beauty by using Zhen Kan to lead me to Christ. Zhen Kan could have died in my womb when I was struggling alone in Brazil during the divorce, or during the long flight back to Malaysia when I was in the 28th week of pregnancy, or during his birth when the umbilical cord was double-looped around his neck. He survived all these. That's why I totally believe in Jesus and am absolutely certain that He is the one true God who rules heaven and earth! God only took him home when his mission was done! Zhen Kan was conceived in Brazil; we left Brazil on August 27, 2011; three years later, we returned to Brazil, arriving exactly on August 27, 2014! I saw God's hand in all these, though it was beyond my comprehension. I deeply believe in this Scripture verse that I bury in my heart, *"Trust in the Lord with all your heart and lean not on your own understanding; In all your ways acknowledge Him, and He will put your paths straight."* (Proverbs 3:5-6)

Proving that Zhen Kan is With Jesus

Shortly after returning to Malaysia, Christ Lutheran Church (CLC) celebrated its 50th anniversary in September. Nina was 5 years old. Before the service started, we were in the crèche. Suddenly, I felt the urge to go out to the sanctuary. The worship singing had just started. Nina ran out to the front, jumping and shouting with joy, *"Yeah! Yeah! Yeah! I found Jesus! I found Jesus! We can bring Zhen Kan home!!!"* I was shocked. She was looking earnestly at Pastor Alex and said, *"I want to fly."* She kept clinging to Pastor Alex as if she wanted him to carry her up and swing her. I told her, "*He's Uncle Alex,*" and she replied, "*It's Jesus, Zhen Kan is there!*" while pointing to the aisle beside Pastor Alex. But there was nobody there. Nina kept fussing and then pointed to the banner with a cross in the front and said, "*Jesus is there, He is going away!*" I thought it was just her imagination. Then, Gillian came over to take her out, thinking that she was disturbing the others.

Two weeks later, Nina told me that she missed Zhen Kan dearly and wanted him to come home. She said, "*Jesus took Zhen Kan to the wrong home, this is our home. If Jesus took Zhen Kan away, he can't find Mama, he can't find Nina and he will cry...*" Nina was crying, and I was crying too. Nina continued, "*It's not Uncle Alex, it's Jesus. He opened one wing, then another wing, and he could fly!*" What?! Did she really see Jesus and Zhen Kan in the church that night? I asked her, "*What's the colour of Jesus' clothes?*" She replied, "*Yellow and black.*" I was wondering if it was real. Shouldn't Jesus be in a white robe? Later, I read the book "*Heaven is for Real*" by Choo Thomas, who was taken to heaven 17 times by Jesus[1]. She wrote that Jesus wore His special golden crown and gown during His birthday and during special celebrations. That would make sense, since Nina did not know the word "gold" yet, so she could only

---

[1] Choo Thomas, *Heaven is So Real*, (Florida: Charisma House, 2003).

describe it as yellow. The black could be due to the dim lighting and spotlight in the hall during the worship singing that had cast the black shadow on Jesus' clothes. That was why Jesus' clothes looked *"yellow and black"* to Nina. I believed Nina had really seen Jesus in the church during the 50th anniversary of CLC celebration. What a privilege for a 5-year-old girl to see Jesus!

I continued to ask Nina, *"What's the colour of Zhen Kan's clothes?"* She said, *"Octopus!"* My jaw dropped. I was stunned because his favourite t-shirt had the picture of an octopus, which he wore for his burial, with the *Car Cartoon* jacket over it. Besides Hemily and me, no one else knew he wore that Octopus t-shirt under the jacket. Hemily was my former husband's relative who helped with the funeral. Everyone else in the funeral only saw Zhen Kan's jacket. I am sure everything that Nina saw was real in the spiritual world. Children do not lie; she is a pure child and totally believes that Zhen Kan is with Jesus in heaven just like I told her in Brazil. I have no doubt that Zhen Kan is truly with Jesus! Not only that, Jesus brought him to visit us and our church during the 50th anniversary celebration!

Besides Nina, Pastor Jennie also testified to me about Zhen Kan being with Jesus. She said that many times, she saw Zhen Kan with Jesus when she was praying for me. She already knew his destiny. Soon after Zhen Kan passed away, I wrote an email to Pastor Jennie, who was then in America. The moment she read my email, she heard an audible voice from Zhen Kan, "*Ma, don't cry!*" She said it was a real audible voice! When Pastor Jennie was sleeping while on her flight back to Malaysia, she saw Jesus holding Zhen Kan's hand again! Zhen Kan looked very happy and healthy, just like before he was ill. Here it is – another proof from his godmother. I have no doubt that Zhen Kan is with Jesus! Hallelujah!!!

How is Zhen Kan Now?

One night, about two weeks after Zhen Kan's passing, I saw him standing at the foot of my bed in my sleep. His face was round and his hair had grown; he was completely different from when he was ill. And he had a big smile on his face. The moment I wanted to call his name "*Zhen Kan*", I woke up and he disappeared. I went back to sleep. I felt it was so real when I saw him! What a precious opportunity to see Zhen Kan even for a short moment! I gratefully thanked Jesus for this special moment with Zhen Kan! Although it was just a fleeting moment, Jesus had given me a very thoughtful and loving gift just when I needed it most. Zhen

Kan's beaming face told me that he was experiencing great joy! He looked absolutely healthy! No more yellowish skin, no more bony body, no more sickness! Jesus said in John 11:25-26, *"I am the resurrection and the life. The one who believes in me will live, even though they die; and whoever lives by believing in me will never die...."* Did Zhen Kan die? Yes, he died a physical death, but he is just sleeping! According to the Bible, his body has fallen asleep in Christ[2] temporarily, while his spiritual being is in heaven with Christ. During the second return of Jesus Christ, Zhen Kan's body will surely rise again, as promised in 1 Thessalonians 4:16, *"For the Lord himself will come down from heaven, with a loud command, with the voice of the archangel and with the trumpet call of God, and the dead in Christ will rise first."* Next, those who are alive will also be caught up together and reunited with the Lord and our beloved. *"After that, we who are still alive and are left will be caught up together with them in the clouds to meet the Lord in the air. And so, we will be with the Lord forever."* (1 Thessalonians 4:17) This is God's promise, a promise from a faithful God who never changes and will keep His word for those who believe in Him. I am waiting with blessed assurance for the

---

[2] 1 Thessalonians 4:13-14.

day of our reunion and eternal life in heaven for an infinite eternity.

Zhen Kan looked exactly like he did in this photo when
I saw him standing at the foot of my bed one night.

Can Jesus Resurrect Zhen Kan Now?

One day, after our return to Malaysia, Nina had a flashback of the time in Brazil when I took Zhen Kan to the hospital without her and she never saw him alive after that. Nina started to cry and said, *"Why didn't you bring me to the hospital? I want Zhen Kan! I miss Zhen Kan so much! I want my baby back!"* Nina kept crying, and I cried too. At that moment, I innocently asked Jesus to resurrect Zhen Kan to demonstrate His power! If Jesus could resurrect Lazarus who was dead for 4 days, surely He could resurrect Zhen Kan. If He is the Son of God, nothing is impossible for Him! I kept praying and asking Jesus to resurrect Zhen Kan! It was like testing Him.

A week later, while driving home along the E23 highway, next to Desa Sri Hartamas, God spoke to me, *"Zhen Kan doesn't want to come back to earth because heaven is a much better place!"* Joy for Zhen Kan flooded me right away! Suddenly I realised that if Zhen Kan was resurrected, he would not be happy growing up with me. He might even become rebellious. His life with Heavenly Father in heaven is zillion times much better than with us on earth. Now, every time I drive along the E23 highway next to Desa Sri Hartamas, I will remember what God has said.

To comfort myself, I found a beautiful painting of heaven, *Supreme Sanctuary* by Akiane Kramarik, an internationally renowned and gifted artist who has visions and visits to heaven. She said, *"In heaven, the colours are more intense, and many of them are not seen on earth. The plants, animals, and all beings speak not through words, but through colour, vibration, and thoughts. Everything is simply beautiful and effortless."*[3] I am eagerly looking forward to heaven.

Will I Jump Down?

There was a period after Zhen Kan's death that a voice would tell me, *"Jump down! Try... jump down here! Probably you can fly"* whenever I was hanging the laundry at the balcony. It was absurd. I knew it was the voice of the devil again and again, tempting me to jump down! When I told my colleague Benjamin about this, he said that it was the same devil (Satan) who tempted Jesus to jump down from the highest point of the temple after Jesus fasted for 40 days in desert[4]. Satan even quoted Psalm 91 to Jesus, that the angels would guard Him and lift Him up! But Jesus answered, *"It is*

[3] https://art-soulworks.com/pages/heaven-is-for-real-painting
[4] Matthew 4:1-6; Luke 4:1-11.

said: 'Do not put the Lord your God to the test.' " (Luke 4:12) This is how Satan attacks us at our weakest moment. Do not be deceived by him, even though he can quote Scripture!

I asked Pastor Francis Ho and Pastor Eric Mau to come over to pray and cleanse my apartment. Still, Satan's evil forces continued to tempt me, but I kept on rebuking them in Jesus' name. I kept praying Psalm 121:3-4, 7-8, "*The Lord will not let your foot slip, He who watches over you will neither slumber nor sleep... The Lord will keep you from all harm, He will watch over your life; the Lord will watch over your coming and going, both now and forevermore.*" Indeed, by God's grace, I did not commit suicide despite Satan's many attempts to get me to jump from my balcony.

The balcony where I fought the devil.

Death Certificate

Sorting out Zhen Kan's death certificate on my own was a pain. It was not a straightforward process because he did not pass away in Malaysia. The process was long and complicated, and I had to deal with several departments. Every step that I took towards getting the death certificate felt like salt was being scrubbed into my wound. The pain in my heart was still raw; it had not diminished since that night when he breathed his last in my arms! How I wished someone could sort out the death certificate for Zhen Kan, but I was all alone. Being a single mother, I must be stronger than all else!

I got the death certificate from the Brazilian hospital and local authority. Of course, it was in Portuguese, the Brazilian national language. I sought advice from the Malaysian Embassy in Brasilia, Brazil. They directed me to a qualified translator to translate the death certificate into English. Then it needed to be certified by the Malaysian Embassy. Back in Malaysia, I went to the Selayang Hospital to get a letter from the doctor to confirm the death of my son. It was not a straightforward single trip but involved a few trips. This was the hospital that I stayed with Zhen Kan before his death, a place of pain and suffering, a place that I had fought and prayed earnestly for his healing. Can you imagine what it's like to have salt rubbed into your raw, bleeding wound? That was how I felt every time I went there!

Once in Selayang Hospital, as I was walking up the long staircase, I asked God, *"What shall I do next?"* Immediately, I heard this word *"mission."* Really? Once again, I knew it was from God because He had always spoken in a subtle voice and in a few words. When there was peace, I knew it was certainly from God, not the devil. It was not from myself because it was not reasonable to go on a mission trip when Nina needed me to be with her. Probably one day in future, I might fulfill the *mission* from God, I figured, and pushed this thought to the back of my mind.

Finally, I got the letter from Selayang Hospital and brought it to the National Registration Department to get the death certificate. Although it had been a long process, I realised that God had been gracious and had watched over Zhen Kan all this while. Zhen Kan did not pass away during the long 30-hour flight to Brazil, nor in Dubai where we stayed two nights. If any of these had happened, it would have been even more complicated to get his death certificate.

Letting Go!

Letting go was indeed very difficult, even though I knew it was much better for Zhen Kan to be in heaven than to suffer here. I drove to work with tears streaming ceaselessly down my cheeks. The tissue paper was my constant companion as tears poured shamelessly at the prayer meetings and worship sessions I attended. My eyes were always swollen red, my face downcast, and my heart heavy. My pain was compounded by the fact that his grave was far away in Brazil. It was too expensive to travel there and how my heart ached. I consoled myself with the thought that it was just as well that his body lay across the oceans, for then I would not be too attached to his grave. Yes, his body is in Brazil, but his spirit is in heaven now, and he is forever in my heart.

I tried to find consolation in watching video sermons on YouTube. There was one particular sermon by Pastor Joseph Prince that lifted me. He said, *"If a child gets a knife, he will think it's shining, sharp, fun to play, and he'll keep holding the knife, and won't want to 'let it go'. Unless someone tells him, he won't know that the knife is dangerous. If his father buys a beautiful toy for him, the child won't be able to play with the new toy until he lets go of the knife!"* This analogy made sense to me. Unless I *"let go"* of Zhen Kan, I will not be able to receive the *"new toy"*, the abundant blessings from my Heavenly Father. If the child insists on holding on to the knife, not only will he not be able to play with the new toy, he might even cut himself with the knife! If I keep on thinking and grieving over my son, I will sink low and will not have space to receive something better from God! The more I let go, the more blessing is on my way. To encourage myself, I always recite Isaiah 43:18-19, *"Forget the former things; do not dwell in the past. See, I am doing a new thing! Now it springs up; do you not perceive it?..."*

The Lord is Close to the Brokenhearted

Although there were church members who supported me during my darkest moments, they could not be with me all the time as they had their own family and work commitments. I totally understand this and cannot expect them to be with me all the time to comfort me. And so, I grieved alone. It was very painful to weep by myself, with no husband there to hold me. There was no one who could share and understand my pain of losing my child.

I cried a lot when I prayed, so much so that once, my torrent of tears flowed to my eyebrows! This happened when I knelt and bowed my head way down low. Instead of flowing down the cheek, my tears flowed to my eyebrows. My worship and prayers were always drenched in tears, even till today. One day, God spoke to me gently and lovingly, "*I know your pain, I know the pain of losing a son... as I saw my Son died on the cross...*" Instantly, I was overwhelmed by God's love. He understood my pain. He had watched His beloved Son die an excruciating death on the cross and He knew exactly how I felt. That very moment, the loneliness lifted from me. I am truly thankful and grateful to God who has saved us through the death of His own Son. In a way, I felt my son sacrificed his life so that I can know Christ. Zhen Kan's death was not in vain. Illumined by this revelation, my heart overflowed with love for God, replacing the fear I had of Him at the beginning. As Psalm 34:18 says, *"The Lord is close to the brokenhearted and saves those who are crushed in spirit."* God has turned my ashes into beauty, mourning into joy, and despair into praise, as He promised in Isaiah 61:3.

One night, I had a dream where I saw a huge book with golden edges. It looked like a very important book, with many names written in it but I could not decipher any names. A magnifying glass appeared and hovered above my name and Nina's name! I woke up with a start, in great joy. My heart was flooded with deep gratitude to God. I fell asleep again in peace. I was a young believer at that time and did not know about the Book of Life. As I diligently sought God and read the Bible, I learned that that book was the Lamb's Book of Life. God has assured me that I will be with Zhen Kan in heaven, as written in Revelation 21:27, *"Nothing impure will ever enter it.... but only those whose names are written in the Lamb's book of life."* What a privilege to have God reveal to me in the darkest hours of my grief that my name and Nina's name are in the Lamb's Book of Life! Hallelujah! Hallelujah!

A year later, on December 23, 2015, two nights before Christmas, I saw Zhen Kan in my dream. We were surrounded by very bright lights. I could not see anything else except him. He looked very happy and grown up a bit more. He said to me, *"I am very happy!"* So was I! I was thrilled to see him even though we did not do anything special. I suppose that must be the eternal joy we will experience, by just being in heaven. God has answered my prayers and let me see Zhen Kan in heaven. He has given me a glimpse of heaven and the blissful joy there. I can never thank Him enough for that precious, comforting insight.

Visiting a Sick Child

One afternoon, Pastor Jennie and I visited Lim Jie Wei, a 20-month-old girl who had been admitted to Hospital Kuala Lumpur for fever and liver issues. Her skin was discoloured and the doctors said they needed to remove a growth in her liver and replace some of her blocked blood vessels. Her liver disorder was congenital, according to the doctor. As I walked into the pediatric ward to visit Jie Wei, I was calm and did not feel emotional at all. When I talked to her mother, Yih Lin, surprisingly I did not cry. I believe that

Yih Lin was encouraged because she was smiling at me all the time that we were with her. Praise the Lord!

I wish to visit children in the pediatric ward, sing and play music, and pray for them in Jesus' name. The first child that I visited had the same sickness and was the same age as Zhen Kan! How coincidental! During Zhen Kan's sickness, I spent a lot of time at many hospitals and was a regular "hospital mother", so it was natural for me to walk into hospitals and talk to the mothers. Although I think of Zhen Kan whenever I go to the hospital, I do not cry. I am very grateful that God has shown me that I have been restored by His grace, and I'm ready to fulfill the mission He has given to me to help other "hospital mothers".

Remembering For Good

I was hungry to know God and I dived into His Word every day to find out the truth. Every Sunday, I went desperately to His sanctuary to worship Him and to seek a fresh encounter with Him. I also watched lots of sermons on YouTube. My hunger to know God led me to sign up for a part-time course at Seminary Theology Malaysia (STM) in July 2016. The first course offered to me was "Missiology"! Wow! I remembered the calling of God (*mission*) in Selayang Hospital. It was not a coincidence, but God's divine plan and arrangement.

One of the courses that I took in STM was "Loss and Grief" in October 2018. It had been four years since the death of my son and yet, it was helpful to re-examine my grief for my beloved son, and re-mend my brokenness. In this course, I did a presentation on planning a funeral for myself! How many people will think of planning and attending their own funeral while they are still alive? The whole planning process caused me to consider my death and funeral, and helped me see life and death from a different perspective. There was also an assignment called *Remembering For Good*, which helped me to re-process my grief, and guided me to live fully after my loss. I would like to share what I've learned.

Remembering For Good[5] is for anyone who is grieving the loss of someone or something important, which could be a person, a pet, an intangible thing like a job or health, or even a dream that has not been achieved but has died even before its birth! Actually, it does not matter how long your loved one has died – a day or 20 years. A loss is

---

[5] Cath Duncan. *Remembering For Good*, www.rememberingforgood.com

still a loss. Your loved one will never be forgotten, regardless of time. There is no direct equation between grief and time. Time is irrelevant after the loss. Grief is not a sickness that needs to be fixed, healed or cured. *"Grief is a natural and healthy response when we love and lose what we love."*[6]

I love my son Zhen Kan very much. When I went through my traumatic divorce in Brazil, he was physically inside me, in my womb. We fought the battle together, all the way from Brazil back to Malaysia. I lost him five years ago when he was only two and a half years old. The loss of my son has caused a further ripple of losses in my life. I lost the opportunity to raise him and see him grow up to adulthood. I lost the opportunity to teach him to read, swim, ride a bicycle, play the piano, cook, etc. I will never see him play with his sister again, and grow up with her. I will never see him graduating from university, nor attend his wedding and cuddle his children. I will not know how he will look like when he is grown up. I can imagine him as a tall, handsome young man with a smashing personality that attracts girls like a magnet. The hardest loss is that I will never see him again in my lifetime. (*It is extremely painful to write this. Can you feel my grief and pain? But these losses are what came to my*

---

[6] Cath Duncan, 14.

mind when I had to do my assignment entitled Remembering For Good!)

After I lost my son, nothing could be worse than my own death. Therefore, nothing distressed me anymore, unlike when I was younger when I would be easily perturbed by the slightest problem. I have released a lot of burdens and resentment I held against people. I also felt "dead" inside, unable to feel and care, and uninterested in life. No words can describe my sorrow and devastation of losing my son. I could not laugh or join in the merriment when I was in the company of cheerful and jovial people. I cried every time I worshiped God. I cried at all the prayer meetings. I cried when I saw healthy children playing happily. Because my son was dead!

After the many losses and countless painful experiences, it would have been very easy for me to close my heart, to not ever love again or desire something, so as to protect myself from potential loss and pain. But closing my heart to avoid loss and pain would mean closing my heart to potential friendships, new love, joy and peace. No, building a thick wall around myself would be very unhealthy. I could either open my heart to live and love fully again or continue to retreat from life and reject every beautiful thing life has to offer. I chose to open my heart. The process towards wholeness did not happen overnight but by the grace of God, I began to live again.

While I was suffering the deep, searing pain of loss of Zhen Kan, I was greatly relieved that I did not have to worry about finances anymore. I had struggled financially to raise two young children on my own, plus additional medical expenses for Zhen Kan. I was also relieved that I did not need to stay in the hospital every month for Zhen Kan's treatment, and take time off from work. And finally, I can give more attention and love to Nina, who desperately needs. Now, I can pour all my love on Nina. I can learn to be a good mother, talk to her, guide her in her studies, and give her my time. I want to be a good mother for my daughter, to give her the best although ours is not a normal family.

Grief has no cure. One just has to learn to live with it, to have a "relationship" with it that will grow and change over time. After five years of losing my son, I have become familiar with grief. There are ups and downs in my relationship with grief. Some days, I am happy that Zhen Kan is in heaven, close to Jesus; other days, I am despondent that he's no longer with me. The emotions in my grief relationship are predictable. His birthday and death anniversary are the hardest times. During the first four years, I grieved deeply on his birthday. Finally, in the fourth year on November 18, I mustered the courage to walk into a cake shop to buy a small cake to celebrate his 7th birthday with Nina. I knew he could not eat the cake, but I really wanted to celebrate his birthday with Nina, who missed him so much. This was one way of processing my grief instead of running away from it. My grief was exacerbated by my singleness, without a husband to hold me during my low moments. Sometimes, I wish I have a man to love me and be with me when I am grieving but if I keep staring at my loneliness, I will sink deeper into my sea of sorrows. Or I can turn to Jesus for His healing love. The two choices are always before me and being human, I often swing between them. But although I am broken, I am still a strong and useful vessel for God, and I allow my grief to propel me to care for the brokenhearted, the single mother, and the grieving mother.

Moving forward, instead of using the word "grieving", I now use "remembering" instead. "Grieving" is perceived as a negative emotion, a cognitive and physical reaction of great sorrow or distress at the death of a loved one. On the other hand, "remembering" allows for the ongoing unfolding and evolving of my story and my relationship with grief, yet without binding myself to intense sadness or sorrow for the rest of my life[7]. "Remembering"

---

[7] Cath Duncan, 18.

also allows me to open my heart to new life and to receive new love, peace and joy. It is a positive feeling, with hope in Christ.

Usually, the people around me, especially my parents, will avoid talking about my son. They have even told my relatives not to query me about him. My friends and colleagues also avoid talking about anything related to my son as they have no idea what to say, and they do not want to see me cry. They think that by talking about my son, I will be reminded of my loss but they do not realise that I remember anyway. If I cry, it is not because they have caused me to remember my pain, but because they care for me and it makes me visible, validated and loved. Another reason that people do not want to talk about my loss is that they hope the loss will come to a "closure". But there will never be a "closure" until I see my son again in heaven. I do not need a "closure", I do not want to forget my son. I do not want to forget all the traumatic times we had been through together, right to the final moment when he left me. *"Closure is the wrong focus and pursuing closure often leads to closed-heartedness. It's safe and healthy to remember your lost loved one. Because remembering doesn't have to be painful. Your remembering can be good for you. Giving yourself and each other permission to remember as long as you do will give you access to gifts and resources beyond your wildest dreams.*"[8]

[8] Cath Duncan, 22.

Chapter 5

A Special Pearl

My Daughter

Although Zhen Kan is the main character in this book, Nina is a big part of the story too. A special pearl, she was one of the main characters who was with me during my grieving moments and has sustained my life, besides Jesus.

I had a miscarriage before I had Nina, hence I was very anxious when I was pregnant with her. My ex-husband and I decided to give her the surname *"Chow Berti"* to represent the bloodlines of both her mother and father. Nina was born in Chesterfield Hospital in the United Kingdom. It was an induced birth as she had refused to exit my womb although the water bag had ruptured more than 24 hours earlier. The labour pangs were the worst physical pain I had ever experienced in my life. I thought I was going to die! How I lived through the intense pain to deliver a healthy baby is something I'll never get over. Women who have delivered their baby normally will understand the labour pain, which is soon forgotten when the baby is placed in their arms. Oh, what joy I felt when I gazed at this tiny baby in my arms, my own flesh and blood. But raising my little bundle as a first-time mother in a foreign country without any help from my own parents and my former parents-in-law was not easy, to say the least.

A Different Destiny

From the UK, we moved to Brazil when Nina was only 9 months old. A baby, she was unaware of the flurry around her. In Brazil, her paternal grandparents loved her very much, and treated her like the most precious pearl in the world, giving in to all her demands. Unfortunately, my marriage did not work out. Nina was only 21 months then when we moved back to Malaysia and again, she did not understand all that was going on. I was absolutely devastated on the day she and I left Brazil. She must have suffered a huge rupture in her love tank since we left Brazil.

When we returned to Malaysia, we stayed with my parents, who had no idea how to express love. I do not blame them as they were the typical conservative, unexpressive Chinese. From a world where she was bathed in love and affection by her demonstrative Brazilian grandparents, Nina entered a bewildering world of Chinese folks who showed no love to her and instead yelled at her when she cried. This made her cry even more. Sensing that she had lost someone or something very precious in her life, she became very insecure and clung on to me like a leach. She was a cranky, fussy child and wailed most of the time. Nobody likes a crying child, especially my parents.

Nina is very similar to her father in both her appearance and character. Her father was diagnosed with ADHD and dyslexia when he was young and was on medication to manage his behaviour. Unfortunately, Nina too was diagnosed with mild ADHD and mild dyslexia. Like her father, she is very stubborn and refuses to follow instructions. Raising a child like her in a normal family is already challenging, so imagine juggling the task of looking after her with caring for a terminally ill son and a full-time job, all on my own.

When Zhen Kan died, I asked God why He took Zhen Kan, who was more like me. Why did he leave me with Nina, who is like her father? Looking at her pained me initially, for she reminded me so much of her father, who had abandoned us. But I kept reminding myself that she did not choose to be born into this family with a Brazilian father and a Malaysian Chinese mother. She did not choose to carry the surname of *Chow Berti*. She did not choose to be born into a broken family. And she did not choose to inherit her father's character and genes. In fact, life has dealt her and Zhen Kan an unfair hand. Both are innocent victims of an irresponsible father who had blazed a trail of disaster and trauma for the family.

It is indeed very challenging to raise and lead Nina back to a normal childhood when she has lost so much, including her younger brother. I keep trying even though I keep failing. I have even been criticised by people for not correcting her or disciplining her with the cane! It has been heartbreaking for me and I have felt condemned many times. These people just have no idea what we have been through.

Encounter with Jesus

One day in November 2016 when we were having dinner at home, Nina asked, *"Can Jesus walk through the wall?"* I replied, *"Yes! Why do you ask?"* Nina said, *"I saw it in my dream. Jesus walked through the wall, I followed Him but I hit my head on the wall. I tried again and again, three times, but I still could not walk through the wall… Then Jesus came back and took my hand and we walked through the wall together to another room."* Wow! What an amazing dream! I have yet to see Jesus in my dream. What a privilege for Nina to see Jesus at this young age (7 years old)! I asked, *"What happened next?"* Nina replied, *"Children were sitting at one table. Zhen Kan, King Yan, Dora, Alicia, Efesus, Charis, Ern Ern, Rowena, Joanna. Daddy and mummy were sitting at another table with Jesus. Uncle Alex was there. We were eating and drinking. Children were drinking grape juice."* She continued, *"Jesus asked me, 'Do you like fish?' "*

Nina told me that Zhen Kan was wearing the white t-shirt with the octopus picture. Again, it was the same t-shirt that he wore for his funeral and the same t-shirt that Nina saw in Christ Lutheran Church during the 50th anniversary service. In Nina's dream, she saw Zhen Kan saying, *"Mama, I want Mama!"* before jumping on to my lap. After dinner, the children played happily while the adults continued talking with Jesus. *"There is another dream where I saw Jesus on the cross,"* she continued. What? Another dream! I was astounded. This was her dream:

There were two soldiers, wearing helmets and red and silver-coloured clothes. They carried long swords and led Jesus to the cross. They nailed Jesus on the cross, one nail on each hand, and one big nail on both legs. There were many stripes on his body and a thorny crown on his head. Jesus was naked. Blood dripped down from His body. The two soldiers stood, one on each side of the cross. Three angels in golden clothes hovered above in the sky. Each had a golden ring above their head and two wings.

When Jesus died, the earth became dark though the sky was still bright. One of the angels was the leader and supervised the other two angels. An angel collected Jesus' blood. Then, they all flew back to heaven. Three large teardrops from heaven fell – one on Nina's head, another on my head, and one more on Zhen Kan's head. They were God's tears. Then, teardrops fell again, one on each of the three of us.

Next, another two soldiers, wearing blue and silver-coloured clothes, took Jesus' body down from the cross and lay His body in the tomb and closed the tomb with a big rock. I cut open the rock with a sword and the three of us went inside and slept next to Jesus' body. Zhen Kan and I hugged our Winnie the Pooh soft toys as we slept. Then, Jesus took us to heaven where we had golden rings floating above our heads, like those above the angels' head. We went into a castle and slept there.

What a wonderful dream Nina had! I believe Jesus loves all the little children, especially a special child from a broken family. And I believe He keeps a closer watch on the children, with His guardian angels always watching over them. "*See that you do not despise one of these little ones. For I tell you that their angels in heaven always see the face of my Father in heaven.*" (Matthew 18:10)

Miracle of Student Pass

When Nina was born, I made a mistake of not registering her birth at the Malaysian Embassy in London. When we returned to Malaysia, I had to apply for her Malaysian citizenship, which was seemingly impossible then. Initially, I applied for the Dependent Visa so that she could stay on in Malaysia. It had to be renewed every year. When she turned 7 years old, she had to get a valid Student Pass (visa) to stay here legally. Every year, I had to sort this out at the Immigration Department – an extra burden.

Due to her special condition (mild ADHD and dyslexia), Pastor Jennie and Ruth advised me to send her to a home school. However, since home schools are not registered with the Ministry of Education and therefore, not recognised by the government, it would be impossible to get the Student Pass if I enrolled her in a home school. I applied for her to get into a government school and thankfully, the application was approved. With this, I managed to get the Student Pass in January 2016, but it was valid for only a year. I was not satisfied with a Student Pass; I wanted Nina to get her Malaysian citizenship. Trusting that God would answer my prayer, I sent her to a home school, School A (not its real name), as it would provide Nina a better learning environment.

A year later, I became anxious and disappointed when there was no news about her citizenship application. I went back to the Education Department and applied to get Nina into a government school. The officer was angry when she found out that I had sent Nina to a home school as that was considered as   misusing the Student Pass. After explaining Nina's condition and showing them the Hospital Selayang appointment card, she calmed down and recommended that I first apply for the "Person with Disabilities Pass" (*OKU – Orang Kurang Upaya*) to get her into a government school for special children. However, after much consideration, I decided to apply for a place at a normal Chinese government-type school. All processes went through smoothly, and my application was approved.

With the new admission letter, I returned to the Immigration Department to apply for a new Student Pass. The officer found out that I had misused the Student Pass! According to the immigration law, the officer could issue Nina a "Certificate of Departure" for her to return to her home country. I was terrified. What else could I do except beg Jesus for a way out. Then I spoke humbly to the officer, explaining our situation and pleading for her forgiveness and a chance to apply for the Student Pass. After listening to me, she went inside to talk to her superior. Miraculously, they decided to let me off for breaking the immigration rule and allowed me to go ahead with the application for a new Student Pass. Phew… thank you Jesus. I cannot imagine being prosecuted for breaking the immigration law! How immensely grateful I was to God for rescuing me! The old Student Pass expired on January 19, 2017. I obtained the new Student Pass the very next day, January 20, 2017! Praise the good Lord! In fact, I could only go to the Immigration Department after getting the school admission letter from the Education Department. If I had got the letter earlier, it would have been more difficult to cancel her old Student Pass at the Immigration Department. And if I got the letter after her

Student Pass expired, I would have other problems with the Immigration Department. Thank God for His perfect timing in renewing the Student Pass for Nina without any major problem. My God is almighty and able to help undo the mistakes I make! Hallelujah!

Miracle of the Malaysian Citizenship

When we returned to Malaysia in 2011, I submitted the application for Nina to get her Malaysian citizenship from the Ministry of Home Affairs (KDN – Kementerian Dalam Negeri). This was an extra battle that I had to fight in the next five years. In the first application, I got the Malaysian Chinese Association (MCA, a Chines-based political party) to support her application. Unfortunately, it was rejected due to the submission of incomplete documents. I submitted the second application in February 2013 and this time around, I had a support letter from Dato Shafei, the UMMO (a Malay-based political party) representative for Wangsa Maju (the area where I lived). Tragically, he lost in the following election and withdrew from politics. Therefore, he could not help me any further.

After I joined University of Malaya (UM) as Senior Lecturer, I talked to Professor Aziz, the Deputy Dean of the Faculty of Engineering. He advised me to write a letter to KDN with the signature support from Professor Hamzah (the Head of Department of Electrical Engineering), Professor Azuan (the Dean of the Faculty of Engineering), Vice Chancellor Professor Amin Jalaludin, and himself. I went to all these bigwigs and got their signature, and personally brought the letter to KDN. Despite all the big names, there was no news from KDN. I went to MCA again to seek their help but they turned me away as there was no MCA representation in KDN. It was most disappointing. Next, a colleague, Ms Goh, introduced me to Pastor Andrew in Seremban, who also worked in a law firm. I went to see him and was assured by his familiarity with how things were done in KDN. He did the necessary but there was no news after several months of waiting. A friend in church, Susan, also tried to help me. She had worked in the Prime Minister's Department previously and knew some government officers there. She made enquiries for me but again, there was no news. Next, she brought me to see an officer, Fauzi, in the National Registration Department, who agreed to help, but remained silent afterwards. A church friend, Beng Fatt, then asked his friend, Steve, from MCA to help. He managed to make an appointment for me to see Mr Chong, the personal assistant to Datuk Wee, the President of MCA, to seek his help.

By now, I was exhausted. I had gone the extra mile to seek healing for my son, yet he died. I was going the extra mile to obtain citizenship for Nina; will it fail too? Once during my prayer time, God told me not to worry because Nina had already got her citizenship in heaven, and she would get her citizenship in Malaysia! I could feel how much God loves Nina. That strengthened me to continue her citizenship pursuit. I asked God what else I could do. He showed me *"The parable of the persistent widow"* in Luke 18:1-8, who persistently went to the judge to grant her justice. As she kept bothering him, the judge, who neither feared God nor cared what people thought, finally granted her justice so that she would stop bothering him. I employed this strategy, and went to KDN personally every month, each time with a new support letter. *"The parable of the persistent widow"* also means that if the unjust judge gave justice to a persistent widow who kept asking, how much more will our God bring justice for His chosen ones who cry out to him day and night.

I searched online and identified the head of the citizenship unit, Puan Norehan Hj Abdullah (Ketua

Setiausaha Bahagian Pendaftaran Negara dan Pertubuhan). I wrote a letter to her, attached with the "Letter of Oath", and took it, along with Nina, to KDN in December 2016. It was the end of the year and nobody was working at the counter. The staff at the next counter told me to go directly to the citizenship unit on the 4th floor of another building. Thanking God for leading us to the exact office, we went there to hand in my letter and documents. Truly, God's favour rests on those who earnestly seek Him!

Then I waited on God for the next step to take. He told me to ask the Vice Chancellor (VC) of the UM to personally write to the Minister of KDN, Dato' Seri Dr Ahmad Zahid bin Hamidi, who was also the then Deputy Prime Minister (DPM). Wow! Let's do it, Lord! I prepared the letter and sent it to the VC and his secretary for the VC's endorsement. I also prepared another letter written by myself to the DPM, supported by the Head of Department, the Dean, and the Vice Chancellor. I brought both letters to the DPM's office and copied the letters to Puan Norehan on January 27, 2017, the eve of Chinese New Year. From December to February, I kept writing emails to Puan Norehan to keep Nina's application on top of her files. Just like the persistent widow, I kept banging on the door.

On February 18, 2017, I received a letter from KDN to collect Nina's citizenship in Putrajaya! Praise the Lord! The Almighty God of heaven and earth had finally opened the door for Nina. Many people had said that getting Nina's Malaysian citizenship was impossible. But Jesus says, *"What is impossible for man is possible for God!"* (Luke 18:27). I brought Nina along to Putrajaya on February 20, 2017 to collect her Malaysian citizenship. It was real! For more than five-and-a-half years I had run around to get this precious document for Nina. When I held the paper in my hand, I could hardly believe it. Finally, Nina has got her Malaysian citizenship. She is now a Malaysian and has every right to stay here legally with me! Zillions and trillions thanks to my Lord Jesus Christ, a miracle-working God who is faithful and true. We do not need to wait for another 10, 15 or 30 years! I do not need to worry about her Student Pass anymore. I could send her to any school. God has answered my tearful prayers, fasting prayers, midnight prayers, dawn prayers, and persistent prayers. Not only did I go all out to fight for the life of my son, I also went all out to fight for my daughter's legal right to live in Malaysia.

God's way is the highest. When I looked to people to help me, nothing happened. There were no references for me to follow. But when God put His idea in my mind and I obeyed His direction, it worked out perfectly! All glory to our awesome God! Hallelujah! Hallelujah! Hallelujah!

Rejection

Nina started her formal education at a home school, School A, when she was 7 years old but she had to stop due to the Student Pass issue. God then opened the door for her to obtain her Malaysian citizenship. Greatly relieved, I took Nina back to School A but they declined to take her back, saying that they could not handle Nina. I understood the school's limitation, that they did not have teachers trained to manage, let alone teach, a special child like Nina. Nina's development would be hindered in this school, I reasoned with myself, to assuage my disappointment. Ah… life is full of disappointments anyway and it must go on.

I had no choice then but to send Nina to the government-type Chinese school. It was going to be an uphill task for her, a special child, to start Primary 2 without the basics in the Chinese and Malay languages. We both struggled with her homework every day. After six months, I decided to send her to another home school, School B. The principal, Ms. F (pseudonym), told me that Jesus forgave people and gave them a chance to change. If Nina could change 0.001%, that would be good enough for her. Unfortunately, the teachers at School B could not handle Nina. Ms. F advised me to send Nina for counselling and sand play therapy in her school, so every week, I took Nina for her therapy class. However, one Tuesday, Ms. F summoned me to her office and said Nina had to leave the school by that Friday! I was shocked and felt she was not gracious enough to give me more time to find another school. I pleaded with her to give Nina some more time as she was attending the sand play therapy sessions, but she did not relent. Getting rejected twice by two schools was like being slapped on both my right and left cheeks. Once again, I had to be sympathetic to the school, that it could not take any more pressure from the teachers and parents who had been complaining about Nina.

I did not give up on Nina's education. I found another home school, School C, which was much further away from our house. They had a special class for special children but the fees were higher. Nina could continue her education but there was a big price to pay – higher fees, long distance and wasted time in the traffic jam sending her to school, then re-routing a long way to my workplace. Nina attended four different primary schools in two years. This not only drained my finances, but the hassle of searching for a suitable school and getting her to adapt to new syllabuses repeatedly had delayed the progress of her studies. I could not imagine the emotional stress she had suffered – moving from country to country, from school to school, and from one loss to another. Nobody could share the burden with me; I could only unload it to Jesus. Though Nina had been rejected by two schools and by many people who did not want her around them, I know one thing for sure – Jesus accepts her and He has given her special encounters with Him to assure us of His special love for a special child.

Special Encourager

When Zhen Kan was sick, I devoted myself fully to caring for him, to the neglect of Nina. After Zhen Kan passed away, I could finally shower all my love and attention on Nina, guiding her in her homework and helping in her character development. She is both my joy and my pain because it is not easy to raise an ADHD and dyslexic child from a broken family. There are days when I am grumpy and moody from the stress of looking after her. One day, Nina lamented, *"I have a happy heart, you have a sad heart!"* That certainly jolted me! She was only 6 years old, yet she sensed my sadness. Zhen Kan had just passed away and I was striving to staying alive. That gentle reminder from my precious 6-year-old was what I needed to perk up from my gloom. My special daughter is my special encourager.

Many times in my dark moments when the evil one whispers suicidal thoughts into my fragile mind, I remind myself that Nina has no one else except me. I should never jump down from the balcony. If not for Nina, I could have died many deaths. From the day Zhen Kan died, I've always reminded myself that my life does not belong to me anymore; it belongs to Jesus, who gave His own life to buy my life and Zhen Kan's life. By God's grace and with His angels watching over me day and night, Nina and I have come so far. I always prayed Psalm 91 to remind myself that *"Nina and I dwell in the shelter of the Most High and rest in His shadow, He is our refuge and fortress... He will cover us with his feathers and under his wings we will find refuge... we will not fear the terror of night nor the arrow that flies by day..."* There is no man in my house to protect us, only God. I tell Nina all the time that Jesus protects us and we therefore need not fear.

I live with Nina alone. There are many times that I want to speak to someone, but I only have her. Sometimes, I talk to her about my woes even though she's too young to understand and share my sorrows. The counsellor who provided sand play therapy to Nina pointed out that Nina was more mature than her age, and she had a richer vocabulary than many children her age. The separation from her father and loss of her brother had left a deep wound in her little heart, which she expresses through her anger. True, she was angry most of the time and this triggered my anger. When I was angry with her, the situation would get worse. I have now learned to control my emotions first, then soothe her by hugging her and telling her "*I love you*", which will calm her and quell her anger. The counsellor tried using the sand play therapy to help Nina to express her sadness through tears – the normal way for release. I pray earnestly for Nina every day, committing her to God. I understand that both my children do not belong to me. If God wants me to take care of Nina, I ask for His wisdom and strength to raise Nina, who is still a very challenging child. Nevertheless, she is the reason that has kept me alive, besides Jesus, and my driving force to continue fighting. *Nina, you are my special pearl!*

9-year-old Nina and Li Sze.

Chapter 6
Loss vs Blessing

A New Creation

"If anyone is in Christ, he is a new creation. The old has passed away; behold, the new has come." (2 Corinthians 5:17 ESV). My past is a traumatic drama of sinful living and suffering. But in Christ, I am now a new creation, with Him at the centre of my life. I actively serve in two children ministries – PowerFun, a Saturday children's programme for the children in the community, and PowerKids, a Sunday school. No longer living for myself, I serve and give my time to the children. Initially, it was painful to see so many healthy and happy children walking into the church when my son was dead. Often, I cried seeing these children but not my

own son there. Why then did I choose to serve these children? It was unbearable and I asked God if I should stop serving there. He immediately answered, *"No! You will see Zhen Kan there."* So, I am still serving the healthy children now. However, I have not seen my son there all these years but now, I understand that what God meant is that seeing those children is like seeing my own son! Another thing I have learned is that being surrounded by the children is part of my healing process and it has helped me to overcome my grief faster.

Jill Austin saw in her vision that *"This great Intercessor was weeping for the lost. His heart was like a wall and inscribed on it were the names of every single human being on earth. He was crying out for each one of these names... The response of His great pain for each suffering person was like a heart attack."*[9] My heart pounded in pain as I read her vision. Although I have started a new life in Christ filled with hope for a better future, and I have been serving the children joyfully, the pain from my loss and the trials in my life remain very real. I prayed and asked God why He did not remove the pain, only to learn that the moment I forget the pain, I will become lukewarm and

---

[9] Jill Austin, *Dancing with destiny: Awaken Your Heart To Dream, To Love, To War.* (Michigan: Chosen Books, 2007), 93-94.

complacent, and sink into my selfish life again. God is using the pain to push me out to serve the lost outside the church.

My life journey has been a roller coaster ride, yet it is necessary to prepare me to carry on a new *"work of the Lord"* for His people and His kingdom. For the rest of my life, I will always remember the prayer I prayed when my son died, *"I do not wish to live for myself anymore, **I give my life to you, Jesus**. I will not chase anything for myself... I will do whatever you tell me to do..."* Wherever God places me, whatever vocation He plans for me, I will obey God in carrying out the *"work of the Lord"* in this lost world. I will lay down my life for the lost sheep that God has entrusted to me. When you have something big enough to die for, you become fully alive.

The Home School Calling

I had achieved my dream career as a lecturer in the University of Malaya, the top university in Malaysia. Nevertheless, I had a burning desire in my heart to do a greater *"work"* for God in reaching out to the lost. This desire was going to be fulfilled in a call to work in a home school, or so I thought.

In December 2015, Pastor Jennie shared with me God's calling for her to start a home school. She saw a vision of me working cheerfully in the school and writing children's books. I did not doubt her vision because I fully trusted her and believed that she really got the message from God. I was very excited about doing this new *"work of the Lord"*, my thoughts absorbed in starting and managing the school while I was still working in the University of Malaya (UM).

On 8 September 2017, I followed Pastor Jennie to the Good Shepherd God of Assembly Church to attend a service by Pastor Bill Wilson, the founder of Metro World Child. During the prayer, I heard a voice, *"You will do what Pastor Bill does... becoming a Christian..."* I interpreted it as *"leading people to Christ like Pastor Bill does, in some ways similar to how I became a Christian."* Unexpectedly, Pastor Bill walked over to pray for me, *"Father, give her strength!"* I was certain that God had called me to work at the new home school. I believed He had entrusted me to pioneer a new era of education for the younger generation, to plant the incorruptible seeds of His Word in their life, to *"train up a child in the way he should go; even when he is old he will not depart from it"* (Proverbs 22:6 ESV), and to lead many parents to Christ indirectly through His school, just like how I got to know Jesus through the Christian kindergarten, GCC.

If I joined the home school, the secular world might see this as a downgrade in my career, social status and salary – from a Senior Lecturer in UM to a principal in a home school. Nevertheless, I was encouraged by Luther who once said, "*I would rather earn ten gulden by a work that is a service of God, than a thousand gulden by a work that is not a service of God but serves only self and Mammon…*"[10]

One of the major considerations for discerning God's vocational guidance is the needs of the world, to help the world become more like what God intends it to be[11]. I saw a need in the Malaysian education, where lots of children were struggling. Bill Wilson wrote, "*the need is the call*"[12]. There was a need for a positive change in the education. I therefore believed this was my "calling". "*…be steadfast, immovable, always abounding in the work of the Lord, knowing that in the Lord your labor is not in vain.*" (1 Corinthians 15:58 ESV). I was thrilled about this "*work of the Lord*" that aimed to raise people to bear the image of the Son[13]. The road ahead

---

[10] David C. Fink, "*Liberating those who work.*" Christian History 110 (2014): 23.

[11] Unknown, "*Calling in the Theology of Work.*" Journal of Markets & Morality 14(1) (2011): 176.

[12] Bill Wilson, *Whose Child Is This? A Story of Hope and Help for a Generation at Peril.* (New York: Metro Ministries, 2012), 106-107.

[13] Peter Orr. "*Abounding in the Work of the Lord (1 Cor 15:58): Everything We Do as Christians or Specific Gospel Work?*" Themelios 38.2 (2013), 208.

would be filled with strenuous work aimed at sharing the gospel to children in their tender age, a laborious work that consisted of evangelism and discipleship, and building up the body of Christ. There were unknown challenges in this new vocation, but I had nothing to fear for I was doing the *"work of the Lord"* (1 Corinthians 16:10). I trusted that God would equip me with new gifts to undertake the new vocation that He was leading me into.

Obedience Met With Disappointment

Pastor Alex and Pastor Jennie have been very successful in running their GCC kindergarten, opening eight branches over 18 years. The kindergarten is their ministry for God in the marketplace, through which they have brought many children and parents to Christ, including me.

For over two years, we prayed and planned for the new home school. Finally, the day came when Pastor Alex called me and told me about his passion in starting the home school for the next generation of children. It was exactly what I had in mind. He named the school after the initial of his three daughters' names, JME (Julynn, Michelle, Eunice). I requested for partnership in this new home school venture; however, Pastor Alex felt it was better that he owned 100%

of the school to facilitate decision making. Although I felt inadequate, I put my whole heart into starting this school for God. I did not mind being employed and taking a huge pay cut. My goal was to build a school where the children would grow strong in the Lord – spiritually, intellectually, physically and socially. It would not only bless my own daughter but every child in the school.

Pastor Alex is a very ambitious man who has unconventional ideas and always does things differently from others. He decided to use the American home school syllabus, Christian Light Education. However, the majority of the international schools and home schools in Malaysia had switched to the IGCSE syllabus by then, as it is widely recognised by the private colleges and universities here. Nevertheless, I was very excited about the new venture, planning everything from A to Z for the home school, including the fee structure, timetable, lesson plans, sports, class activities, arts and craft, field trips, daily Scripture memory verses, and most importantly, the *Character First* programme that uses Bible stories for the children's character development. The school started off with only three children, including Nina. It was an all-encompassing job, where I taught 7 hours a day, including teaching all the subjects, class activities and sports. Lunch was with the children, so there was no break. Working long hours with the children every day was like running a never-ending marathon, compared to working in UM where I only taught 3 hours a week. I kept telling myself that I could do all things through Christ who gave me strength (Philippians 4:13). I gave my all to the children, thinking that I was laying down my life for them. I kept encouraging myself with John 10:11 (KJV), *"I am the good shepherd: the good shepherd giveth his life for the sheep."* As Jesus is the Good Shepherd who laid down His life for us, I could also do it by His strength.

Pastor Alex and I gave our best to JME in every way to get the school going. We prayed earnestly every day without ceasing. Yet, the number of students did not greatly increase and some students dropped out instead. Towards the end of the second year, Pastor Alex decided to close the school as it had recorded a big financial loss. It was a huge disappointment for both of us as we felt we had obeyed God in starting the school. I had sacrificed much, given up my career in UM and I might not be able to work there again. This was another harsh reality that left me perplexed about God's plan. Once again, my heart grieved over another loss. Yet, I still trusted God, leaning on Him alone, and praying Proverbs 3:5-6, *"Trust in the Lord with all your heart and lean not on your own understanding; in all your ways acknowledge Him, and He will put your paths straight."*

Some of us might have experienced disappointments in life in doing His work and left the church or even left Him. It is a greater loss if you leave God when you are at the bottom of the valley. You will not be able to walk out of the valley on your own strength and will. We are mere humans, made of flesh and blood. Frail and weak, we are easily swayed by the evil forces and influences of the world. We are assailed on every side by greed, fame, envy, prosperity, hatred, insecurity, fear.... The spiritual warfare in this world is intense, especially in this digital age of information overload and social media. Without God, we will be easily drawn into this world's web of deceit without even realising it. Without God, there is no way we can live in peace and joy. When I have Jesus in my life, even when my obedience to Him is "rewarded" with disappointment, I will not fall; I can stand firm in God and believe that He has a greater plan for my life. God loves me, and His next plan is definitely bigger and better than building this school for the children.

When my son passed away, my heart was in deep anguish but I did not walk away from God because I knew He loved me. When my daughter was rejected by the schools, my heart grieved but I did not walk away from God because I knew He loved me. Now, the school, which I had poured my soul into, was closed, and my heart again grieved but I did not and I will never walk away from God in any difficult circumstance because I know God truly loves me and He will work out something even better for me as promised in Romans 8:28, "*And we know that in all things God works for the good of those who love him, who have been called according to his purpose.*" What I needed to learn in this experience, I have learned; what I needed to do, I have done. The experiences in these two years are not wasted but will prepare me for the next phase of my life for God. I don't know why the school did not succeed, but I believe the reason will be revealed at the right time.

Career of Passion

After two years away from the academia, I lost my confidence in securing an academic position in a university. I prayed earnestly and asked God for direction. Through it all, I knew I needed to follow my passion and my God-given gifts. As written in Romans 12:6-8, "*We have different gifts, according to the grace given to each of us. If your gift is prophesying, then prophesy in accordance with your faith; if it is serving, then serve; if it is teaching, then teach; if it is to encourage, then give encouragement; if it is giving, then give generously; if it is to lead, do it diligently; if it is to show mercy, do it cheerfully.*"

Teaching is my gift and passion. I realised this years ago, which was why I completed my PhD. I had sacrificed my career in UM to answer the call to work in the home school. Now was the time to return to the university. Since I love teaching and learning, the best place for me is none other than academia.

When one door closes, God will open another door with bigger opportunities. As long as we fully trust God and stand firm in faith, God will not let us down. God will surely work out His good purposes for those who love Him. He answered my prayer beyond my imagination when I was offered the Assistant Professor position at the UCSI University in January 2020. It was the first choice in my list of potential employers. When I first entered the UCSI campus, I saw the large sculpture of a bird's wing spread open above the entrance gate and a large bronze plate with the inscription, "*Glory to God. For from God and through God and to God are all things. To God be the glory forever.*" It is Romans 11:36! The UCSI University logo is a stylised wing of a bird in flight to symbolise its dynamism and visionary aspirations to soar to great heights of achievements, in line with Isaiah 40:31, *"but those who hope in the Lord will renew their strength. They will soar on wings like eagles…"* I was so touched when I realised that God had brought me to a missional university even before I knew that the founder Dato' Peter T.S. Ng is a Christian.

Although there are new challenges, new subjects, new research ahead of me, I rejoice that I can fulfil and use my God-given gifts and talents. I enjoy lecturing and teaching youths and most importantly, inspiring them. Just as William Arthur Ward said, *"The mediocre teacher tells. The good teacher explains. The superior teacher demonstrates. The great teacher inspires."* The most famous physicist, Albert Einstein, said, *"Education is what remains after one has forgotten what one has learned in school."* At the end of the semester after the final examination, it is normal for students to forget what they've learned. Therefore, I always inspire them with good values, which I hope will remain with them for the rest of their life. I am so grateful that I am now back in the academic marketplace for God and the next generation.

Majestic wings hover above the entrance of UCSI University.

Romans 11:36 in the UCSI University campus.

Treasure on Earth

As Jesus taught in Matthew 6:24, *"No one can serve two masters. Either you will hate the one and love the other, or you will be devoted to the one and despise the other. You cannot serve both God and money."* Although I have an absorbing job, I keep reminding myself that God is in my top priority. In John 15:5, Jesus says, *"I am the vine; you are the branches. If you remain in me and I in you, you will bear much fruit; apart from me you can do nothing."* Without Jesus, I can do nothing or achieve anything on my own strength and intelligence.

During the second month of my new job, I received a phone call one day, allegedly from the court, accusing me of owing a furniture company, registered in Johor, RM18,000. I told the woman on the other line that there was no such thing and she said she would transfer the call to the police station to make a police report. Then, a man, supposedly a police officer, took over the call. He accused me of being involved in money laundering and drug trafficking, and reminded me that it carried the death penalty in Malaysia! The phone was passed from one "police officer" to another and the interrogation dragged on for several hours. By now, you would have probably guessed it was a scam, but I didn't know any better then. They fooled me, a naïve simpleton. I had been living by faith financially in the past two years while working in the home school and did not have much saving. But the scammers managed to withdraw all my housing loan repayment amount of RM40,000 from my bank loan *Flexi* account, and even withdrew RM9,200 from my credit card! I utterly regretted my stupidity and ignorance and had many sleepless nights. Even though I had prayed during the phone conversation, I fell for the scam! My finances were down to zero, plus I had a credit card debt for money that I did not even spend!

This time, my heart grieved over my financial loss. Did I walk away from God? No! Did I lose faith in God? No! Did I question God? Yes, and He promptly told me, "*Do not store up for yourselves treasures on earth, where moths and vermin destroy, and where thieves break in and steal. But store up for yourselves treasures in heaven, where moths and vermin do not destroy, and where thieves do not break in and steal. For where your treasure is, there your heart will be also.*" (Matthew 6:19-21) God reminded me to be generous in giving to the poor and the needy when I have money. Otherwise, the money will be gone in one way or another for any expected or unexpected reasons. Everything that we have – whether material possession, career, children, spouse, family, health, social status and friends, everything – all belong to God. He gives and He takes, sometimes for reasons that we cannot comprehend with our human mind.

God allowed Satan to crush Job to the extent that he lost everything, including all his possession of 7,000 sheep, 3,000 camels, 500 oxen, 500 donkeys, and a large number of servants. He even lost all his seven sons and three daughters[14]. Not only that, Satan went further and afflicted Job with painful sores from the soles of his feet to the top of his head[15]. Yet, Job remained steadfast in his faith and love for God, never cursing and sinning against God despite his wife's egging him to curse God.

Furthermore, Job's three friends – Eliphaz, Bildad and Zophar – who initially came to comfort Job, ended up judging and condemning him. The first friend, Eliphaz, rebuked Job, *"Who, being innocent, has ever perished? Where were the upright ever destroyed? As I have observed, those who plow evil and those who sow trouble reap it."* (Job 4:7-8) The second friend, Bildad, reprimanded him, *"Surely God does not reject one who is blameless or strengthen the hands of evildoers."* (Job 8:20) The third friend, Zophar, drove the hammer further down, *"if you put away the sin that is in your hand and allow no evil to dwell in your tent, then,*

---

[14] Job 1:1-3.
[15] Job 2:7.

free of fault, you will lift up your face." (Job 11:14-15) Their condemnation and judgement were so lengthy that they lasted from chapter 4 to 25 in the book of Job. Their conclusion was that God sent calamities on wicked people to punish them for their sins. Even I, have asked myself if I have sinned so badly to deserve all these "punishments" and brokenness in my life. Although there are cases where God punishes the wicked (as in Sodom[16]), God does not always work that way. In the story of Job, God clearly condemned Eliphaz when He said, "*I am angry with you and your two friends, because you have not spoken the truth about me, as my servant Job has.*" (Job 42:7) Here is a priceless lesson of wisdom: Do not assume that troubles are the signs of God's judgement! When the disciples asked Jesus in John 9:2, "*Rabbi, who sinned, this man or his parents, that he was born blind?*" Jesus replied, "*Neither this man nor his parents sinned, but this happened so that the works of God might be displayed in him.*" (John 9:3)

Another priceless lesson is that of friendship – when a friend is hurting due to some problems, do not jump into the conclusion that he/she has sinned. Do not ask him/her to confess the sin and repent, because we might not know the whole picture, and we do not know God's plan for him/her.

---

[16] Genesis 19:1-29.

Instead, we should *"mourn with those who mourn"* (Romans 12:15), care for the hurting person like Jesus cares for you. Be willing to enter into the pain of a suffering friend by providing any form of support and comfort. You can only do this genuinely when you are clothed with the love and compassion of Jesus.

In the story of Job, despite all his losses – including all his possession and children, physical pain, criticism from his wife, and condemnation from his friends – he stood firm in his faith. Indeed, *"There is no one on earth like him: he is blameless and upright, a man who fears God and shuns evil."* (Job 1:8) Thankfully, Job had a happy ending: *"The Lord made him prosperous again and gave him twice as much as he had before."* (Job 42:10)

Do not be discouraged if any troubles or problems assail you. Look at me – I am a little "Job" and I can testify that despite all the painful trials I have experienced, we can still stand firm in faith and continue to love God. God has even prepared me before the phone scam incident through a sermon by Pastor Philip Tan two weeks earlier. He preached about financial restoration in three testimonies, where God restored up to 2 folds, 4 folds and even 7 folds to what has been stolen. Has God restored me? No! Will God restore me? Yes! But it will be in His own time and in His own way. No matter what happens, I will remain steadfast in faith, still praying Proverbs 3:5-6. I continue to trust in the Lord with all my heart and will lean not on my own understanding even when my heart is grieving over one loss after another because I know that a grieving heart is most loved by God. "*The Lord is close to the brokenhearted and saves those who are crushed in spirit*" (Psalm 34:18). When my heart is grieving and when I am alone, I pray Psalm 73:21-26:

> *21 When my heart was grieved*
>
> *and my spirit embittered,*
>
> *22 I was senseless and ignorant;*
>
> *I was a brute beast before you.*
>
> *23 Yet I am always with you;*
>
> *you hold me by my right hand.*
>
> *24 You guide me with your counsel,*
>
> *and afterward you will take me into glory.*
>
> *25 Whom have I in heaven but you?*
>
> *And earth has nothing I desire besides you.*
>
> *26 My flesh and my heart may fail,*
>
> *but God is the strength of my heart*
>
> *and my portion forever.*

Indeed, God is the strength of my heart and my life. There is nothing on earth that I desire besides God. He is my portion now, forever and in eternity.

Chapter 7

Forgiveness

Forgiveness from Above

A year after the death of my son, when I was still a young Christian, I attended the Jesus Festival conference where one of the speakers was Pastor Philip Mantofa. In his sermon, he shared the story of the Samaritan woman who met Jesus at the well[17]. I have a secret – I have a past similar to that of the Samaritan woman. Nobody knew this secret, except Jesus. He knew all the past relationships that had deeply wounded me, including relationships with an Iraqi man, a married man, and Mr. L. Like many women, I had

---

[17] John 4:4-26.

longed for a fairy-tale relationship, but none had worked out. When I realised the first two relationships were wrong, I steeled myself to break off the relationship although it broke my heart. When I realised Mr. L was not Mr. Right, it was too late. I suffered the seemingly endless ripples of consequences of marrying that irresponsible man.

At the Jesus Festival conference, I wept a lot during the worship sessions as Jesus' immense love enveloped me. Jesus assured me that He had forgiven all my sins and freed me from all the chains, bondages, grudges, bitterness and brokenness. I felt Jesus telling me that He had forgiven me of all my sins. That was a conviction I desperately needed, for the weight of my sin was too heavy. He lifted my burden. He spoke to me just like He spoke to the Samaritan woman, *"Everyone who drinks of this water will thirst again, but whoever drinks of the water that I shall give him will never thirst; the water that I shall give him will become in him a spring of water welling up to eternal life."* (John 4:13-14) I no longer desire the things of the world that will not satisfy my thirst. Jesus has filled me with His *living water*, a spring of water that will never cease flowing for eternity. This *living water* is the eternal joy that flows from my heart with the blessed assurance from Jesus that nothing can take it away. This *living water* is an indomitable strength deep within me that helps me overcome any challenges and difficulties in life. This *living water* is the eternal hope in Christ in any hopeless situation. This *living water* will nourish me with God's unconditional love, which will bless the poor, the weak, the brokenhearted and the lost.

In the story of the Samaritan woman, after Jesus spoke to her, "*… the woman left her water jar, and went away into the city, and said to the people, 'Come, see a man who told me all that I ever did. Can this be the Christ?' They went out of the city and were coming to him.*" (John 4: 28-30) She left her water jar! Yes, she left the vessel that was to help fulfil her purpose for going to the well because she was overjoyed to find the Messiah, the *living water*. She had something more important than drawing water from the well. She was willing to stop what she was doing and run back to the city to tell everyone about Jesus. She could not wait. She had earlier left the city in the afternoon to go to the well to draw water to avoid seeing anybody because of her shame. But after the divine encounter with Jesus, she ran into the city immediately to share the good news. She had no shame, not even after Jesus revealed she had had five husbands and the man she was living with was not her husband. She was liberated from her painful bondage of shame after Jesus spoke to her. Jesus filled her with the love that she had never experienced before. And she knew that Jesus had truly forgiven her sins. She could stand tall and speak boldly for Jesus. God transformed a sinful and shameful Samaritan woman into a bold and confident evangelist! Her testimony was powerful, for "...*they went out of the city and were coming to him.*" The people in the city also put down what they were doing and went out of the city to see Jesus. There is an amazing *magnetic* power when a woman testifies for Jesus. "*Therefore, there is now no condemnation for those who are in Christ Jesus, because through Christ Jesus the law of the Spirit who gives life has set you free from the law of sin and death.*" (Romans 8: 1-2) Jesus had set her free! And Jesus has also set me free from all my sins and shame! He has given me courage and confidence to write, to testify and to speak for a living God who loves you.

Why am I disclosing my shameful secret? Because there may be many women struggling with dishonourable relationships like I did before. Jesus loves you. You deserve a much better man for your life. Each of you is very beautiful and very precious. Do not compare yourself with others. Do not let any man despise you, manipulate you, and use you for his selfish agenda and personal desire. You are made in the image of God, you have a wonderful purpose and calling to bring joy and love to the people around you. Your existence deserves a much better purpose than indulging in the fairy tale fantasy. Even if you are single like I am now, there is a purpose. God is calling you. Just open your heart to Him. Spend time listening to Him. Be willing to leave your "water jar", to leave what you are doing to fulfil His plan! I left my "water jar" – my job as Senior Lecturer in UM – to answer His call to teach at the home school. Even though it didn't work out, I still believe that it was part of His plan. God has restored my dream and passion by opening a door to a marketplace missional university to continue His plan for His Kingdom. *Are you ready to leave your "water jar" to answer His call?*

Forgiveness from My Heart

When Mr. L decided to divorce me, his parents brought us together for a talk. Although I did not fully understand Portuguese, I could make out that his mother was urging him to divorce me since he did not love me anymore. I was very surprised by the Brazilian way of settling marital unhappiness without considering the plight of the innocent children. Facing the divorce all alone in Brazil was a torturous experience. On the day I left Brazil with Nina in

2011, I made up my mind never to get in touch with the Berti family again. I wanted to cut them off completely from my life.

But as you know by now, when Jesus came into my life during my son's illness, my life changed. By the grace of God, I have forgiven my former parents-in-law and resumed my relationship with them. My former parents-in-law have regretted all the pain and struggles I went through because of their son. They supported me financially when my son was very sick. My former mother-in-law has changed and she now loves Nina and me. She often sends us clothes and presents all the way from Brazil. My former father-in-law even paid for the renovation of my apartment in Malaysia! Forgiveness not only brought healing to our relationship, it opened a door of unexpected blessings in our life.

Will you forgive Mr. L if you were in my shoes? He had snuffed the life out of me, crushed me to nothingness. It was not possible for me to forgive him at first, not until Jesus came into my life. Jesus emptied me and filled me with His divine love and unspeakable joy. From a proud, independent woman, He has transformed me into a little child who trusts and depends completely on her Heavenly Father. As Jesus has forgiven me, He continues to fill me with His power and strength that slowly transform my heart to forgive Mr. L.

"Bear with each other and forgive one another if any of you has a grievance against someone. Forgive as the Lord forgave you." (Colossians 3: 13) It is indeed God who forgives us first; then only do we have the capacity to forgive others. It does not work the other way round. If you try to forgive someone on your own in order to seek forgiveness from God, you will continue to struggle.

Although Mr. L and I are divorced, he ought to share the responsibility for our daughter, especially her education. Although the Brazilian judge had ordered him to support us financially, he managed to free himself from this obligation. He got married soon after the death of our son and he now has a son. Since the divorce, I have tried my best to manage all the financial expenses on my own. But after the phone scam, I had a big financial hole and a debt to pay! Bad things often come in torrents. After the JME home school closed down, Nina attended a few schools before I found one that would accept her but I could not afford the high fees. Who could I turn to? No one else but Jesus. I prayed earnestly, I sought Him for guidance and wisdom. My heart was grieving… Out of the blue, God spoke to me and told me to apologise to Mr. L. What???!!! I had already forgiven him, but God was telling me to apologise to him! I wept and I cried out to God, not knowing how I was going to do that. As

I continued praying, I realised that I was not the only one who had suffered from the divorce. He had also suffered a lot of emotional pain from the broken marriage. Then, I did not even dare ask him if he was having an affair because I was too afraid to know the truth, and I did not want to deepen my wounds. When I brought Zhen Kan and Nina back to Brazil in 2014, he did not have the courage to come and see his own son in the hospital. And of course, he was trying to avoid his family's condemnation by not attending his son's funeral. If you were in his shoes, you too might not have the courage to attend the funeral. I do not know if he has even forgiven himself for missing the only chance to see his own son before he died. Perhaps he was trying to avoid the unbearable emotional pain. I was very sad when his mother told me that he had cut off ties with her. No doubt he is struggling and lost. He needs Jesus in his life.

After much prayer and thought, I finally wrote an email to Mr. L. Here is an extract of the email:

> *I know our marriage was a very hurtful experience until you came to a decision to divorce me. It's very hurtful and bitter for both of us. Unfortunately, the children are the victims. I must admit that I was not a perfect wife, I have never been a perfect person. I*

made many mistakes and I have many weaknesses. For all the things that I have hurt you, here I am, I want to sincerely apologize, I am sorry. I am truly sorry to hurt you. I hope you can forgive, because I believe it will help both of us to carry equal responsibility for Nina.

In my email, I wrote about all the struggles and damage that Nina had gone through since the divorce, the rejection by many schools, and the loss of her brother. If you are a single mother, here is my humble advice – if you can, let the father of your children share equal responsibility in paying for their expenses. Do not burden yourself by doing everything on your own, just because you hate that "man". Forgive and let go. Blessing will flow forth into your life when you forgive.

When God told me to write this chapter on *Forgiveness*, Pastor Francis Ho preached on *Forgiveness* on the day I was planning to write the chapter! It was not by chance, but God's divine plan. Pastor Francis preached, *"Forgiveness is a gift to yourself, a key to freedom. Holding a grudge does not make you strong; it makes you bitter. Forgiving does not make you weak; it sets you free. The weak is not able to forgive; forgiveness is the strength of the strong. We forgive a person not because he or she deserves it, but you deserve to have peace and blessings when you forgive. If you do not forgive, you leave your wound open. But the moment you forgive, healing takes place, and you will definitely be happier and healthier physically and mentally."* Praise the Lord for giving me the strength to forgive Mr. L. Not only did I forgive him, I even asked him for forgiveness for all the hurt he had been through. This is only possible by the amazing grace and love from Jesus. Praise the Lord!

Chapter 8

Most Loved

Discernment

I was once a self-centered, stubborn, egoistic and proud woman. But I hit the pit, stripped off almost every material thing I owned, including husband, house, car, savings, career, and son. The perfect Scripture verse to describe how I feel now is Philippians 3:8, *"I consider everything a loss because of the surpassing worth of knowing Christ Jesus my Lord, for whose sake I have lost all things. I consider them garbage, that I may gain Christ."* All the material things that I have lost are only temporal; none can compare to the eternal life that I have gained in Christ. Though it was not my choice to know Christ this way, I am very grateful He chose me to be His, to receive His unmerited and undeserved grace.

Everything that has happened has a purpose. *"He would deconstruct what is flawed in order to reconstruct what is wholesome."*[18] God has emptied and humbled me so that I can follow, submit, and fully obey His direction for me to be part of His greater plan for the salvation and reconciliation of His Bride to the Bridegroom and His children to His Kingdom. I am one of His chosen broken vessels to reach out to this broken world, which is desperately searching for the truth but still trapped in the endless cycle of sin and death. My journey in this life has been a series of pain, loss and disappointment. But all these have helped me to write this book. Just like Apostle Paul said, *"I have become all things to all people, that by all means I might save some."* (1 Corinthians 9:22b ESV) I have no worldly achievement to boast about except my pain, losses, difficulties, challenges and hardships. Just like Apostle Paul said, *"Therefore I will boast all the more gladly about my weaknesses, so that Christ's power may rest on me. That is why, for Christ's sake, I delight in weaknesses, in insults, in hardships, in persecutions, in difficulties. For*

---

[18] Voon Choon Khing, *Discerning God in Our Life: The Dance of Two Wills*. (Seremban: Seminari Theoloji Malaysia & Genesis Books, 2016), XXII.

when I am weak, then I am strong." (2 Corinthians 12:9b-10). In all my many difficulties, God has said to me time and again, "*My grace is sufficient for you, for my power is made perfect in weakness.*" (2 Corinthians 12:9a) As God has comforted me in all my troubles and affliction, I can now comfort those in any trouble with the comfort I have received from God[19].

As I discern the purpose of my life, it is not just about making a particular choice or plan in my life, but "*discernment is about a way of life in relationship with our Lord God.*"[20] Our Lord Jesus desires to have a very special and unique relationship with each of us, far more than we can comprehend, simply because He loves each of us in a very special way. Without prayer, there is no discernment. I desire for a more intimate relationship with Jesus each day and therefore devote every morning to seeking Him, reading His Word, and eagerly waiting to hear Him. I have a burning desire to fellowship with Him and fully engage Him every day. Every moment spent with Jesus invigorates and excites me, and sets the tone for my day. Even experiencing His love in little things will move my heart toward Him. There are no words to express the joy of sweet communion with Him. As I

---

[19] 2 Corinthians 1:4.
[20] Voon Choon Khing, 111.

experience His amazing love and grace in my life, I fall deeper and deeper in love with my Saviour. *"The mystery of the Gospel is the mystery of a divine, eternal love story between the Bridegroom and the Bride. God is calling for His Bride – for you."*[21] My most favorite verse for prayer is none other than *"Love the Lord my God with all my heart and with all my soul and with all my mind and with all my strength."*[22] Jesus is more than the Lord of my life, He is also the Father to my daughter and my Protector[23], as well as my Bridegroom King. I am willing to faithfully follow my Bridegroom King every step of the way for the rest of my life. And I long to be in His arms to dance with Him, to answer His call and to fulfill the purpose that He created me for.

Baton of Faith

I was honoured and blessed to serve in the Lutheran Church of Malaysia (LCM) Pastor Leadership and Children Ministry Conference in 2018, organised by Pastor Alex and Pastor Jennie. During the first day of the conference, August

---

[21] Jill Austin, 16.
[22] Mark 12:30, Luke 10:27, Matthew 22:37, Deuteronomy 6:5.
[23] Psalm 68:5 (ESV).

23, Pastor Bill Wilson preached about "making a difference" from the story of Moses and Aaron. Thousands of people were dying in the wilderness as they sinned against God. *"Then Moses said to Aaron, 'Take your censer and put incense in it, along with burning coals from the altar, and hurry to the assembly to make atonement for them. Wrath has come out from the LORD; the plague has started.'"* (Numbers 16:46) Without a second thought, Aaron did exactly what Moses said. He ran to the altar to get the fire (the burning coals), then he ran into the midst of the assembly, he offered the incense and made atonement for them. *"He stood between the living and the dead, and the plague stopped."* (Numbers 16: 48) Yes, Aaron made it! He was an old man who had his own problems like any of us. Yet, he obeyed, he took action, and he made a difference as he stood between the living and the dead! One person can make a difference! I can make a difference when one person reads my book. You can also make a difference in many different ways!

After the first day of the conference, in the middle of the night, I was awoken by an "alarm" ringing repeatedly and these words came to me: *"Make a difference! Run to the altar! Make a difference! Run to the altar! ..."* It was 1:00 a.m. and I could not return to sleep, so I fell to my knees to pray. Even when I tried to sleep later, I lay awake till morning came. I just prayed throughout the whole night. God reminded me of the night Zhen Kan passed away. Pastor Bill had preached on Isaiah 6:1, "*In the year King Uzziah died, I saw the Lord seated on a throne, high and exalted, and the train of his robe filled the temple.*" I was extremely devastated when I lost Zhen Kan and everything in my life but that night, I recognised the sovereign God of the whole universe. I knew God was calling me to "*Make a difference! Run to the altar!*"

The following weekend, the LCM conference was held in Ipoh. It was August 30, the death anniversary of Zhen Kan. I was very blessed and spiritually nourished by another series of preaching by Pastor Bill Wilson. My soul danced and rejoiced over his messages that encouraged my soul. During one of the sessions, he used the analogy of a baton in a relay race in his sermon on Hebrews 11-12. There was a relay of faith from Noah, Abraham, Isaac, Jacob, Joseph, Moses and many other characters in the Old Testament. In our time, the baton of faith was handed down by the reformers, evangelists, Martin Luther, Billy Graham and Pastor Bill himself. Using the analogy of a 4 x 100m relay, it is crucial that every runner runs the lap without dropping the baton and passing the baton to the next runner. No matter how good or how fast the first few runners are, it will not be completed until the last runner finishes the race. Similarly, no matter how great the characters in the Old Testament and New Testament were, the race is not complete without the next generation carrying and passing on the baton of faith. I read with alarm the words of Hebrews 11:39-40, *"These were all commended for their faith, yet none of them received what had been promised, since God had planned something better for us so that only together with us would they be made perfect."* The faith can only continue to the next generation if someone is willing to sacrifice, to take the baton, to carry on the faith to finish the race. Only together with the next generation can all that has been done by the forerunners of faith be made perfect!

Pastor Bill expressed his concern for the younger generation, whether they will continue the race in Christ. He asked if anybody wanted to take the baton, but nobody responded. He continued to preach and asked again. I was waiting to see if anybody wanted it but nobody responded. My heart was pounding as I wanted to get the baton though I had no idea what to do and how I was going to do it. All I knew was that four years ago on that day (August 30) when Zhen Kan passed away was the day I gave my life to Jesus. I had no reservation; this was the moment, the defining moment in my life to get the baton from Pastor Bill. If he asked again, I would raise my hand. As I was busy writing the notes, I missed the third time he asked! I told myself, if he asked again, I would not miss it. Paying full attention to every word he spoke while writing and waiting for the moment, he asked again! Immediately I raised my hand. He said, *"You want it, come out and get it!"* I stood up and stepped out to get the baton from Pastor Bill. I said, *"Thank you"*.

It was no coincidence but God's divine appointment that I gave my life to Jesus on August 30, the day I lost my son. I had declared then that I would not live for myself but for God. On this very same day four years later, I took the baton from Pastor Bill to carry on his passion and love for the younger generation and lost souls. The baton is just a symbol. All of us are qualified to carry the baton of faith to our children, grandchildren and the people around you. *"… let us run with perseverance the race marked out for us, fixing our eyes on Jesus, the pioneer and perfecter of faith."* (Hebrews 12:1-2) Just as Paul said in Acts 20:24, *"I consider my life worth nothing to me, if only I may finish the race and complete the task the Lord Jesus has given me – the task of testifying to the gospel of God's grace."* Because of His grace, I am living today and testifying to you through this book.

A Grieving Heart is Most Loved

Without Zhen Kan, I would have been a lost soul. My little boy was abandoned and rejected by his biological father when he was only three months old in my womb. He might not even have been born. The chance of a miscarriage was high, considering all the trauma that we both went through during the pregnancy. But God sustained his life long enough to fulfill his mission to lead me to Christ. What a noble mission given to my precious little boy! I realise that God will do whatever it takes to lead His children to His Kingdom. God has sacrificed His one and only begotten Son for our salvation. I realise how much God loves me and my family even before we know Him. I am proud of Zhen Kan for being part of God's plan in saving my family. He is a little boy who carries the mission for the salvation of the entire family and the generations to come. He will always be honoured in my heart.

Many people have asked the same question – if God loves us, why does He allow sickness and death and not answer our prayers? Why does He allow pain and hardships in our life? There are many purposes and reasons, as written in this book. One of the reasons is to encourage you, the reader, to continue to put your faith and hope in Christ in any difficult circumstances or even in hopeless situations. Despite grief and pain, we can still live with joy and strength because we are filled with the *living water* from a living God. Hardships and difficulties will never crush you, but they will make you stronger and tougher. In good and bad, I trust God with Proverbs 3:5-6, and confidently believe in Romans 8:28, *"And we know that in all things God works for the good of those who love him, who have been called according to his purpose."*

Again, my life is like Philippians 3:8-11 ESV, *"Indeed, I count everything as loss because of the surpassing worth of knowing Christ Jesus my Lord. For his sake I have suffered the loss of all things and count them as rubbish, in order that I may gain Christ and be found in him, not having a righteousness of my own that comes from the law, but that which comes through faith in Christ, the righteousness from God that depends on faith - that I may know him and the power of his resurrection, and may share his sufferings, becoming like him in his death, that by any means possible I may attain the resurrection from the dead."*

"I consider that our present sufferings are not worth comparing with the glory that will be revealed in us."

(Romans 8:18) I am looking forward to the day of Jesus' second return, to witness His glory. As written in 1 Thessalonians 4:16, *"For the Lord himself will come down from heaven, with a loud command, with the voice of the archangel and with the trumpet call of God, and the dead in Christ will rise first."* I am waiting for the day to witness the resurrection of my son. I believe this day will come to pass in my lifetime because I had a dream where I was lifted up above the earth with my child. I was looking down and saw fire everywhere on earth. It was the final day of judgement! God will restore and renew everything and *"He will wipe every tear from their eyes. There will be no more death or mourning or crying or pain, for the old order of things has passed away. He who was seated on the throne said, 'I am making everything new!'"* (Revelation 21:4-5) God will restore everything in the Holy City, the New Jerusalem, which is also the New Heaven and New Earth. And we will dwell in the *Shekinah* presence of God with all our loved ones in eternity.

I like to end my book with my favorite daily prayer taken from the Song of Mary (Luke 1:46-50):

My soul glorifies the Lord, and
   my spirit rejoices in God my Savior,
for he has been mindful

of the humble state of his servant.

From now on all generations

> *will call me blessed,*

for the Mighty One has done great things for

me,

> *Holy is his name.*

His mercy extends to those who fear him,

> *from generation to generation.*

If you are grieving for whatever reason or loss in your life, I am here to tell you in the name of Jesus, ***A Grieving Heart is Most Loved*** by God! To God be the glory!

Epilogue

If you have been moved by my testimony and you long to experience the love of Jesus, please invite Jesus into your life. Pray this prayer, in your heart or out loud, *"Dear Lord Jesus, I invite You into my life as my Lord and Saviour. I am a sinner, and I ask for Your forgiveness. I believe You die for my sins and rose from the dead. Thank you for Your forgiveness and giving me a new life. I want to trust You and follow You. Fill my heart and my life with Your eternal love, peace and joy. I love You Jesus. In Jesus' name I pray, Amen!"*

If you wish to know more about Jesus, you may write to me at **lisze.chow@gmail.com**.

Bibliography

Austin, Jill. *Dancing with destiny: Awaken Your Heart To Dream, To Love, To War*. Michigan: Chosen Books, 2007.

Duncan, Cath. *Remembering For Good*, **www.rememberingforgood.com**

Fink, David C. "*Liberating those who work*." Christian History 110 (2014): 20-25.

Orr, Peter. "*Abounding in the Work of the Lord (1 Cor 15:58): Everything We Do as Christians or Specific Gospel Work?*" Themelios 38.2 (2013): 205-214.

Thomas, Choo. *Heaven is So Real*, Florida: Charisma House, 2003.

Unknown, "*Calling in the Theology of Work*." Journal of Markets & Morality 14(1) (2011): 171-187.

Voon, Choon Khing, *Discerning God in Our Life: The Dance of Two Wills*. Seremban: Seminari Theoloji Malaysia & Genesis Books, 2016.

Wilson, Bill. *Whose Child Is This? A Story of Hope and Help for a Generation at Peril*. New York: Metro Ministries, 2012.

www.ingramcontent.com/pod-product-compliance
Lightning Source LLC
Chambersburg PA
CBHW051833150726
47998CB00001B/403